Are We Ready?

Helen Reed

Distributed by New Wine Press
PO Box 17
Chichester PO20 6TJ

Unless noted otherwise, Scripture quotations are taken from the
New King James Version of the Bible. Copyright 1979, 1980,
1982 by Thomas Nelson, Inc.

Scripture quotations marked KJV are taken from the King James
Version.

Scripture quotations marked NIV are taken from the Holy Bible,
New International Version. Copyright 1973, 1978, 1984 by
International Bible Society.

J.B. Phillips, *The New Testament in Modern English*. Copyright ©
J.B. Phillips 1960, 1972. HarperCollins Publishers, Glasgow.

Where parts of Scripture quotations are in bold type, the
emphasis is the author's own.

ISBN 1 874367 97 3

Typeset by CRB Associates, Reepham, Norfolk.
Printed in England by Clays Ltd, St Ives plc.

Contents

Acknowledgements

I want to thank our wonderful Lord Jesus Christ for His love, for His mercy and for His faithfulness, and for all the people He has brought into my life who have helped, encouraged and prayed for me and for this book. I especially want to thank Michelle Castro-Vieira for all her help with the computer; and Chris Thomas, Anna Davies and Joan Piper for their help and advice. Special thanks also go to my wonderful husband, Doug, for his love, help, support, patience and input without which this book would never be in print.

Preface

Nearly everybody is wondering what is going to happen in the future. Now, more than ever. In fact, almost all the Christian books in the American 'Top Ten' are about the 'last days'. Here is another one – but rather than majoring on what I think is going to happen and my interpretation of the Bible prophecies, I want to focus on how to **prepare** for the last days; not so much in a practical sense, but how to be ready **spiritually**, for whatever may happen and whenever it may happen, and ultimately, how to be ready to meet Jesus.

This may also be seen perhaps, as a warning to those who think they are alright as well as those who know they aren't – in fact it is a warning to all of us including myself. I do not want to be a 'doomsday prophet' or to be negative and I certainly don't want to put condemnation on anybody. Please don't put this book aside after only reading the first few pages, saying 'There's no hope for me'. Rather, let this be a **challenge** to each of us to make sure we are ready, and also an **encouragement**, remembering that our wonderful Lord Jesus knows our hearts and our desire to be right with Him.

Will we be ready? Will we be able to cope with the difficulties we may have to face? I believe that if we are ready spiritually, many of the practical issues will also be taken care of.

In showing how we can prepare for the last days there are two main areas that I want to talk about, which are inter-related and inter-dependent. The first, which is the most important, is having an intimate love relationship with Jesus and I will endeavour to show you how I came (and am still coming) into this relationship. If it is possible for me, it is also possible for you. I am no different from you! The second, which stems from that relationship, is living by faith, and by relating some of my own experiences I pray that you will be encouraged and that your own faith will be strengthened. In between these two sections I have inserted a part which deals with maintaining our relationship with Jesus and also some of the hindrances. There is no point in developing that relationship if we can't keep it once we've got it! All the way through, I have tried to illustrate from my own personal experience to make it more interesting and hopefully, something you may be able to relate to.

If you already have a wonderful relationship with Jesus, then perhaps this will be a challenge to go even deeper. There is always more – we can never say we have arrived! Even as I write this I am crying out to Jesus to bring me into an even deeper, ever more intimate relationship with Him. It is not just 'pie-in-the-sky' that I am talking about but down-to-earth, practical ways of living and walking in peace and joy with Jesus, in the victory He purchased for us on the Cross. Even if some of the things that the Bible foretells and men are predicting, do not happen in our life-time, we still need to be equipped and able to cope with the difficulties all of us may have to face sometime in our life. Even more importantly, we need to be ready to meet Jesus, either when we die physically, or when we are *caught up* (raptured) . . . *to meet the Lord in the air,'* (1 Thessalonians 4:17).

As you read the following pages, may I encourage you to reach out to Jesus and ask Him to reveal Himself to you; ask Him to reveal His love and His faithfulness, in a new and deeper way than you have ever known before. He will – because that is the kind of prayer He loves to answer. Above all I pray that we will all fall in love with Jesus afresh so we can be a part of His bride who *'has made herself ready,'* (Revelation 19:7).

INTRODUCTION

The Last Days

The telephone rang one morning and as I answered it, the sound of a friend's voice came excitedly over the wires.

'Helen! You **must** read this book! You've **got** to read it! It's so wonderful! I'm so excited! I want to come and give it to you this afternoon. Is that OK? Oh, you really **have** to read it!'

'Well, OK. What's it about?'

'It's about Jesus coming back! He's coming very soon! This man says there's going to be a mighty outpouring of the Holy Spirit at the Feast of Tabernacles in Jerusalem next year. That's going to be the beginning of the Tribulation. I'm going to go to Israel to be there!'

The more my friend spoke, the more excited she became. And it certainly sounded interesting. After she had left our home that afternoon I looked at the book she had placed on the table. It was very thick, about 400 pages. I glanced through it quickly, wondering how this man could be so sure the seven years Tribulation was going to begin at that time and exactly when Jesus was going to return for the Christians. My Bible told me we would not know the day or the hour.

Over the next few months I slowly read the book. I checked all the Bible verses the author used and everything he said, and I couldn't find anything to fault him on. The author's reasoning for Jesus to come back at a certain season of a specific year was very convincing and logical. He was careful not to specify the day or the hour, knowing that the Bible clearly states that we will not know those details, but he was very specific about the month and the year, and when he thought the Tribulation would begin, which was only a matter of months from then.

After I had finished reading the book I was asking the Lord Jesus what He wanted me to do and how He wanted me to prepare for that time, **whenever** it might be. In my mind I was thinking that this preparation could include many things, perhaps even moving location. But Jesus showed me so clearly that the preparation He wants me to make is to **develop my love relationship with Him**. Those words that Jesus spoke into my thoughts were so clear and I knew it was so necessary. I am still aware how essential it is, not just for me but for all of us. If we can do nothing else to prepare for the last days, all of us can concentrate on developing our love relationship with our wonderful Lord Jesus, the Lover of our souls!

When my husband, Doug and I were in England in January 1999, we found so many people were talking about Y2K and the millennium bug. Some churches were encouraging their members to stock up on canned food, kerosene and candles, and others were talking about digging cess-pits in case the water and sewage system failed. Later we heard that some people in America were leaving the cities, building homes in the country, digging wells, stockpiling food to last two or three years, and even buying guns in case a shortage of food causes hungry mobs to riot.

Soon after that we were in the Philippines, a developing country, and even in the remote villages where many have never even seen a computer, the question on everybody's lips was, 'What's going to happen in the year 2000? Is this the beginning of the last days? Will we be raptured before trouble starts?' It seems that those who had television had seen programmes talking about the problems that may be caused by computers failing. They, in turn, had told others, and everybody was wondering if their world was going to collapse. The fact that none of them had computers, some did not even have electricity, they already pumped their own water or had wells, and many grew their own fruit and vegetables and raised chickens and pigs, meant that they, in fact, were far better equipped to cope with any of the possible scenarios that experts were predicting, than people in the western countries where we rely on computers to control almost everything! (By the time you read this 1 January 2000 will have passed so we will all know what happened on that day!)

We had been invited to speak at a three-day convention and were told that the topic was 'The Millennium' and we were to talk on Revelation 20:1–6. As we sought the Lord beforehand, we felt that He did not want us to talk about what we thought was going to happen. There are so many differing interpretations of Scripture, so many opinions and predictions, and we did not want to add our 'two-penny worth'. Many people think all the 'Christians' will be 'raptured' (caught up to heaven) before the seven years of Tribulation. Others think only some Christians will be raptured. Some believe that all the Christians will have to go through the whole of the Tribulation and then be raptured. Yet others feel the Christians will be raptured in the middle of the Tribulation, after the first three-and-a-half years. We must always stay open to what the Lord Jesus may say to us concerning this and beware lest our minds be like concrete – all mixed up and set!

I would be very happy if we were raptured before the Tribulation and I do not rule that possibility out.

9

However, from what I have read throughout the Bible, I feel that we born-again, Spirit-filled Christians will have to go through some, if not all, of the Tribulation. I do not want to go into that in depth because there are many other books that deal with that subject. Suffice it to say, there are several scriptures that give me the impression that we will still be around when things get bad. In Matthew 24:6–13 Jesus is talking to His disciples (see verse 3). Are **we** His disciples today? If we are, He is also talking to us. He says,

> *'And you will hear of wars and rumours of wars. See that you are not troubled; for all these things must come to pass, but the end is not yet. For nation will rise against nation, and kingdom against kingdom. And there will be famines, pestilences, and earthquakes in various places.'*
> (Matthew 24:6–7)

[In the two months prior to this date, 20th October 1999, there have been two major earthquakes in Turkey, one in Greece, two in Taiwan, one in Mexico and another one in California!]

> *'All these are the **beginning of sorrows**. Then they will deliver you up to tribulation and kill you, and you will be hated by all nations for My Name's sake. And then many will be offended, will betray one another, and will hate one another. Then many false prophets will rise up and deceive many. And because lawlessness will abound, the love of many will grow cold. But he who endures to the end shall be saved.'*
> (Matthew 24:8–13)

Verses 21–22 continue,

> *'For then there will be great tribulation, such as has not been since the beginning of the world until this time, no, nor ever shall be. And unless those days were shortened, no flesh would be saved; but for the elect's sake those days will be shortened.'*

10

Before I go on, maybe I should say who the elect are. The Bible says,

> 'If you confess with your mouth the Lord Jesus and believe in your heart that God has raised Him from the dead, you will be saved.'   (Romans 10:9)

All of us who have asked Jesus to forgive our sins ['For all have sinned and fall short of the glory of God' (Romans 3:23)], and have asked Him to be **Lord** of our lives, are the elect. When we ask Jesus to be Lord of our lives, it means we are asking Him to come into our lives and take control. We are promising to do whatever He tells us to do and go wherever He tells us to go, whether or not it is convenient and whether or not it is something we want to do! We do not belong to ourselves anymore, we belong to Jesus: 'For you were bought at a price' (1 Corinthians 6:20), 'with the precious Blood of Christ' (1 Peter 1:18/19).

Also in Matthew 24 Jesus says,

> 'Immediately **after** the tribulation of those days the sun will be darkened, and the moon will not give its light; the stars will fall from heaven, and the powers of the heavens will be shaken. **Then** the sign of the Son of Man will appear in heaven, and then all the tribes of the earth will mourn, and they will see the Son of Man coming on the clouds of heaven with power and great glory. And He will send His angels with a great sound of a trumpet, and they will gather together His elect from the four winds, from one end of heaven to the other.'

(Matthew 24:29–31)

It certainly sounds as though we, the elect, will still be around during the Tribulation, otherwise Jesus would not have said the angels will gather us together **after** the Tribulation! Despite the number of earthquakes, famines, and wars in the world, I am not saying we are in the Tribulation now, but surely these are the 'beginning of sorrows.'

11

2 Thessalonians 2:1–4 says,

> '. . . let no one deceive you . . . that Day (the rapture) will
> not come unless a falling away comes first, and the man
> of sin is revealed . . . '

That sounds like we will be here to see the Antichrist, sitting in the temple.

You will notice that I have spelt Tribulation with a capital 'T'. That is to distinguish that specific period of seven years from any other tribulation that all of us may go through. Jesus Himself said we would have tribulation in John 16:33,

> 'These things I have spoken to you, that in Me you may
> have peace. In the world you will have tribulation; but be
> of good cheer, I have overcome the world.'

Some people, however, may have to go through more tribulation than others and unless we are prepared, we may not be able to cope with it.

We heard a true story of a pastor in China who, many years ago, taught his church members that they would be raptured before the Tribulation. Then communism took over and the Christians were persecuted. That pastor fled to Taiwan but many of his flock were imprisoned and many more were killed. Years later, when things were much easier, the pastor thought he would return to his village in China and find out how his fellow-Christians were doing. As he walked down the road he saw an old man he recognised and went up to him. The old man took one look at him and ran away. Puzzled, the pastor went to talk to a woman he recognised. This woman also looked at him with horror on her face and ran away. This happened several more times until the pastor stopped another man who started to run away. He grabbed hold of his arm quickly: 'Please don't run away. I'm pastor so and so. Don't you remember me? Why does everybody run away from me?'

The man replied, 'Yes, we remember you. But you told us we'd be raptured before the Tribulation and look what we've been through. We weren't prepared to go through all this persecution. You're a false prophet!'

Over the years, and even as I write this, many Christians are being persecuted and are suffering for their faith in many different countries all over the world. We heard a pastor preaching that the Christians were 'not appointed to wrath' and a few minutes later he said approximately 100,000 Christians had been killed in Rwanda, Africa in recent months. That was certainly wrath or tribulation for them! In *Our Globe And How To Reach It* (1990, Barrett & Johnson) it says that 9.9 million Christians were martyred in the past forty years. That's an average of nearly 250,000 every year! As I have just quoted, Matthew 24:9 says,

> *'Then they will deliver you up to tribulation and kill you, and you will be hated by **all** nations for My Name's sake.'*

What makes us think **we** will be the exceptions? Why do we say to ourselves, 'That will never happen where I live. I'm sure **I'll** never have to go through any persecution.' But maybe we **will** be persecuted. Isn't it better if we prepare ourselves beforehand, just in case?

Apart from that, if we live carelessly, there is even the possibility that we could **miss** the rapture, whether it is before, during or after the Tribulation! There are books on the market now which teach that those who miss the rapture will have a second chance. But can we be sure of that? Four times in the book of Revelation it says that the people who were not killed by the various plagues during the Tribulation *'did **not repent** of their deeds'* (Revelation 16:11 with 9:20–21 and 16:9). We must not be lulled into thinking there will be a second chance in case there isn't. **Now** is the time to make sure we are ready.

Proverbs 29:18 says,

> *'Where there is no revelation, the people cast off restraint.'*

The King James Version puts it,

> *'Where there is no vision, the people perish.'*

Another version says,

> *'Without a progressive revelation, the people live carelessly.'*

We may think we are alright; living a morally upright life, not hurting or criticising other people, going to church regularly, and praying before we go to bed at night. We may be active in the church, teaching Sunday School or leading the worship. Perhaps we are on the mission-field, working night and day to bring the Gospel to the unreached. Or do we wonder if it is even necessary to be so 'fanatical' about religion as long as we are born-again? But if we put these different versions of Proverbs 29:18 together we get the impression that if we do not continually have a fresh revelation of Jesus we live carelessly, doing whatever we want, and this causes us to perish and die spiritually.

So what does it mean, to have a fresh revelation of Jesus? What does it mean to have any revelation?

PART ONE

Relationship

Chapter 1

Knowing and Being Known

To have a revelation of something is to know something supernaturally. There is a natural knowing and a supernatural knowing. I am sure all of you reading this book know about Jesus. You have heard about Him from your parents or teachers or friends. Perhaps you go to church and hear about Him every week. But do you actually know Him?

I was brought up in a Jewish family and therefore did not hear about Jesus from my parents. I was not allowed to attend the Scripture lessons at school but in my early years I occasionally found myself in one by mistake when the teacher forgot to tell me I should go and sit outside. If I did hear the Name of Jesus mentioned I would immediately think, 'Oh dear! I shouldn't be here,' and start to panic. So His Name was somehow related to something wrong! Later on during my school years I frequently heard His Name used as a swear-word so that did not give me the right impression either! But if anybody had asked me if I knew Jesus, I would probably have replied that I'd heard about Him. I hardly knew anything about Him and I certainly did not know Him.

Later, when I was hitch-hiking through Europe, I met some Christians who told me that Jesus loved me so much that He died for me. This so amazed me that I started reading the New Testament they had given me and I began to know more about Jesus, but I still did not know Him personally. It was only after I asked Jesus to forgive my sins and come and live His life in me that I began spending time with Him and really getting to know Him. It was some time after that that I suddenly knew that I **really** knew Him and that He was very real to me! Although I cannot see Jesus, He is as real to me as the chair I'm sitting on. Over the years since I first asked Jesus to take control of my life I have gradually got to know Him even better. As I have spent time with Him, talking to Him, reading the Bible and repeatedly asking Him to help me to know Him better, every now and again it has been as though a light was switched on inside me and I've suddenly **seen** something new about Jesus. I've had a **revelation** of His love for me, of His grace, of His faithfulness. I have suddenly seen what a wonderful Friend He is, *'a friend that sticks closer than a brother'* (Proverbs 18:24), which to me is very special because I have a brother who is very close to me and Jesus is even closer than that! I have seen Jesus as the great *'I AM'*. Jesus IS! Whatever I need Him to be at any particular moment, Jesus is! My wisdom, my righteousness, my strength, my Provider, my Shepherd, my everything! As we ask Jesus to reveal Himself to us, He will. And I believe He continually wants to give us fresh revelation, a deeper revelation of Himself as we ask Him and yearn for Him.

Any friendship that is going to last, however, is not just one-sided. When I was a teenager I would sometimes meet a boy that I thought I would like to get to know. If he did not want to get to know me, however, that was the end of that! Making friends is a two-way thing. Any close relationship has to be mutual. I could ask you if you know the Queen of England, or some other well-known personality, and you would probably say yes. But if I ask you if the Queen knows you, you would more than likely say no! We can know somebody without having any relationship with them. It is the same with our relationship with Jesus. We can know Him, but does He know us?

There are several passages in the Bible that show us how important it is for Jesus to know **us**. The story of the ten virgins is one of them. Matthew 25:1–13 says,

*'Then the **kingdom of heaven** shall be likened to ten virgins who took their lamps and went out to meet the bridegroom. Now five of them were wise, and five were foolish. Those who were foolish took their lamps and took no oil with them, but the wise took oil in their vessels with their lamps. But while the bridegroom was delayed, they all slumbered and slept. And at midnight a cry was heard: "Behold, the bridegroom is coming; go out to meet him!" Then all those virgins arose and trimmed their lamps. And the foolish said to the wise, "Give us some of your oil, for our lamps are going out." But the wise answered, saying, "No, lest there should not be enough for us and you; but go rather to those who sell, and buy for yourselves." And while they went to buy, the bridegroom came, and **those who were ready** went in with him to the wedding; and the door was shut. Afterward the other virgins came also, saying, "Lord, Lord, open to us!" But he answered and said, "Assuredly, I say to you, **I do not know you**." Watch therefore, for you know neither the day nor the hour in which the Son of Man is coming.'*

All of these were virgins. We could say that all of these were born-again Christians. But there were five of them to whom the Bridegroom (Jesus) said He did not know them. How can that be if they were Christians? Perhaps we can argue that they were not active Christians; they were not doing any good works for Jesus. So let us look at another passage in Matthew 7:21–23.

*'Not everyone who says to Me, "Lord, Lord," shall enter the **kingdom of heaven**, but he who does the will of My Father in heaven. Many will say to Me in that day, "Lord, Lord, have we not prophesied in Your name, cast out demons in Your name, and done many wonders in Your name?" And then I will declare to them, "**I never knew you**; depart from Me, you who practice lawlessness!"'*

18

In both of these passages it is Jesus who is speaking and in both of them He is talking about the kingdom of heaven. Jesus is saying that certain people will not enter the kingdom of heaven because He never knew them! That means He never had a **meaningful relationship** with them! That, to me, is very challenging! Does Jesus know **me**? Does He consider that He has a meaningful relationship with **me**? 1 Corinthians 8:3 says,

'If anyone loves God, this one is known by Him.'

What does it mean to love God? Jesus Himself said,

'He who has My commandments and keeps them, it is he who loves Me. And he who loves Me will be loved by My Father, and I will manifest Myself to him . . . . If anyone loves Me, he will keep My word; and My Father will love him, and We will come to him and make Our home with him.' (John 14:21–23)

Loving Jesus means we do the things He asks us to do, not the things that **we** want to do. To love somebody means we want to please them, and that person will respond. When we love Jesus we want to please Him and He responds by revealing Himself to us in a deeper way and He fellowships with us – He says He knows us and we have a two-way meaningful relationship with Him, an intimate relationship with Him.

Matthew 7:13–14 says,

'Enter by the narrow gate; for wide is the gate and broad is the way that leads to destruction, and there are many that go in by it. Because narrow is the gate and difficult is the way which leads to life, and there are few who find it.'

Will we be one of those few who have a meaningful relationship with Jesus?

Chapter 2
Relationship

Whether you and I are ready for the end times, and are ready to meet Jesus when we die or when He comes for His Bride, largely depends on our relationship with Him.

What kind of relationship do we have with Jesus? Is it the kind of relationship that there is between a master and a slave, or a boss and an employee where we are told what to do and we have to do it or we will get beaten or lose the job? Do we feel that if we do not do what Jesus tells us to do He will not love us anymore or we will lose our salvation? Are we afraid that if we do something wrong He will not speak to us anymore?

Is it just a nodding acquaintance like we may have with somebody we see on the bus or train on our way to work everyday? Do we just say hello to Jesus on a Sunday morning or before eating a meal?

Is it the kind of relationship we may have with a lawyer or a doctor whom we only go to when we have a problem? Do we only talk to Jesus when we are in trouble or get sick? Do we stop talking to Him again when He has solved the problem or we get well?

Is it like we would have with a friend who we chat to on the telephone once a week or have coffee with occasionally? Do we only talk to Jesus when it is convenient or when we don't have anything else to do?

Is it like the friendships little girls sometimes have when they see each other everyday and tell each other their secrets – but after a few months they make new friends and don't have time for each other anymore? When we first met Jesus did we speak to Him all the time and read His Word everyday – but after a few months we got too busy, other things were more important and we gradually stopped talking to Him?

Is it a kind of selfish relationship where we hope the other person will make us happy and meet our need to be loved and we expect them to do all we ask, but we don't really care how they are feeling and are not prepared to go out of our way to do anything for them? Do we expect Jesus to do all we ask Him to do but we do not want to know what is on His heart and are not willing to ask Him what He wants? Do we want Him to satisfy all our needs but we are not interested in satisfying Him?

Or is it the kind of meaningful relationship that people dream of? A two-way, mutual relationship of love and commitment? One where we meet somebody who we can trust implicitly, commit ourselves to totally and know they are committed totally to us. Someone with whom we can share our hopes and aspirations and not feel they will laugh at us. One whom we can tell everything, even the very worst about ourselves, and not be afraid they will stop loving us. One with whom we can share all that is on our hearts and want to know what is on their heart. That somebody who we know will always love us unconditionally and we accept that love and respond to it by wanting to please them. We know they understand us and will never leave us. One who cares for us, is always there for us, and wants to help us with all our problems – nothing is too big and nothing too trivial for them to be interested in. Is that not what we **all** want?

> *'What a man desires is unfailing love.'*
>
> (Proverbs 19:22, NIV)

We think what joy there would be, what security, what comfort, to know that we are loved with such an unfailing love.

My friend – our relationship with Jesus can be any one of the above. It depends on us. Jesus has no favourites. He has already shown us how much He loves each one of us. He died for us.

21

> *'Greater love has no one than this, than to lay down one's life for his friends.'* (John 15:13)

Such love! There is no fear that we may do something wrong or say something that will stop Jesus loving us or make Him leave us.

> *'Perfect love casts out fear.'* (1 John 4:18)

Such wonderful love!

> 'No other love could be so amazing;
> So vast, so patient and free.
> He accepts us, and draws us, close to His side;
> And we can rest – in the joy of His security.'
> (*O Lord You Are So Mighty* by Marilyn Baker
> – copyright Word UK)

The warmth, the security of His arms of love surrounding us!

And it's a **gift**. We cannot **earn** it. We cannot do anything to make Jesus love us more than He already does. He just loves us because He loves us because He loves us – because He *loves* us!

But we **can** become more aware of His love by accepting it and by responding to it. The Song of Solomon is one of my favourite books of the Bible because it shows me the love Jesus has for me – and for you.

> *'My Beloved is mine, and I am His.'* (2:16)

> *'I am my Beloved's, and His desire is toward me.'* (7:10)

Jesus says to me,

> *'Behold, you are fair, My love . . .*
> *You are all fair, My love . . .*
> *You have ravished My heart . . .'* (4:1, 7, 9)

Isn't that almost too much to believe, that we could ravish Jesus' heart?! But that is what He says and each of us can choose what we do with those words. We can choose to ignore them; we can choose to believe they only apply to the 'good' Christians; or we can mix them with faith and choose to believe that Jesus is talking to us!

Paul prayed that

> '[we] *may be able to comprehend with all the saints what is the width and length and depth and height – to know the love of Christ which passes knowledge; that* [we] *may be filled with all the fullness of God.'*
>
> (Ephesians 3:18–19)

Really **knowing** the love of Jesus causes us to be filled with all the fullness of God! Wow!

So how **can** we know that love? How can we know that vast, that perfect love of Jesus if it **passes** knowledge?

I believe we can only get a glimpse of it but that that glimpse can get bigger. Our finite minds certainly cannot understand it or work it out. Our hearts are too small to contain it. But King David knew the One who was able to enlarge his heart:

> '*I will run in the way of Your commandments,*
> *For You shall enlarge my heart.'*   (Psalm 119:32)

He knew because he had experienced that enlarging for himself.

> '*Thou hast enlarged me when I was in distress.'*
>
> (Psalm 4:1, KJV)

When we get a small glimpse of the vastness of Jesus' love for us, it feels like our hearts could burst. But if we ask Jesus to enlarge our hearts, maybe it will mean we must go through some distress! Before we pray that prayer we need to decide if we **really** want to know more of Jesus' love! Are we willing to pay the price? Those who have been through distress and clung to Jesus in the midst of it, have come out the other side with a deeper knowledge, a deeper experience of His love. And they have been filled a little more with the fullness of God.

There are some people we meet, not very many, who shine with the beauty of Jesus. It is not a physical beauty. It is the fullness of Jesus that shines through them. If we spend time with these people and get to know them, we will find they have been through many trials and distresses in their lives. They have truly been broken, allowing the beauty of Jesus to shine through. They have committed their lives a hundred per cent to Jesus. They have given themselves to Him in the same way that He gave Himself for them. They have been willing to 'lay down their lives' for Him!

I have a husband who loves me. I **know** he loves me. And I know he loves me with the love of Jesus because it is an unconditional, unfailing love. Our marriage has been through some tests and trials. At first I thought, 'Oh, he'll not want anything to do with me after this.' But I found I was wrong. He still loved me. In fact, the more tests and trials we went through, the more I experienced the depth of his love for me – and my love for him. Now I **know** that he loves me and will always love me. And there is a joy and security in that. We have a really close relationship that did not just happen overnight. We have had to work at it, and are still working at it. It has developed over the years through the things we have been through together, being honest with each other, sharing with each other how we feel and talking through our differences.

At our wedding, when we said the marriage vows, we committed ourselves to each other, 'for richer for poorer, for better for worse, in sickness and in health, till death us do part.' That was a promise we made to each other before God. We should not break that promise. When we went through a difficult patch in our relationship a few months later, we recommitted ourselves to each other to remind ourselves of what we had promised. We do it each time we go to somebody else's wedding – not because we need to but because we want to. We want to be totally committed to each other and we do almost everything together – not because we have to but because we choose to.

I am particularly blessed. Not only do I have a caring, godly husband, who loves me unconditionally, but I also have a friend who loves me. Even though this friend now lives thousands of miles away, I know she's there, she's praying for me and she cares. I could call her at any time if I needed her help and she knows that I care for her in the same way and would do anything to help her. How did this friendship come about? We spent hours talking to each other, opening up and being honest with each other. We did not put on a mask and pretend to be better than we were. We did not try to cover up what we were feeling when we were going through difficulties in our lives. We did not say 'I'm fine' when we were not. I am not saying we should go round telling everybody our problems, but it is wonderful when there is a special friend we can be real with, and who can help us find Jesus in the situation.

Jesus wants us to have an even **closer** relationship with Him. Not only does He want us to know how much He loves us but He also wants us to accept His love and respond to that love. He wants us to spend time with Him, talking to Him, listening to Him speaking to us in our thoughts and through His Word each day. We can open up and be honest with Him, telling Him how we feel, good or bad. He knows anyway, but He wants us to tell Him. Jesus wants us to fellowship with Him. We are **called** to have fellowship with Him!

> *'God is faithful, by whom you were called into the fellowship of His Son, Jesus Christ our Lord.'*
>
> (1 Corinthians 1:9)

The more we spend time with Jesus, the more we will get to know Him and the more we will love Him. And the more we love Him, the more we will want to spend time with Him and the closer we will want to be to Him. We will also want to **please** Jesus! Selfish love wants to be pleased. Unselfish love wants to please. If we want to please Jesus, we will want to obey Him. To obey Him means we need to know what He wants us to do – which means more time spent with Him, fellowshipping with Him, developing our love relationship with Him. It means a commitment.

At this point some people may say they do not have time to spend hours with Jesus – they are too busy. I am not talking about hours shut away in a prayer closet. There are some who can do that, and that is wonderful, but the majority of us must make do with an hour or so each day, praying and reading the Bible. What I am talking about is fellowshipping with Jesus all day long – wherever we are and whatever we are doing. We can talk to Jesus as we get washed and dressed in the morning, and as we travel to work or take the children to school. There are a lot of things we do where our minds are free to talk to Jesus. Many times our work demands our full attention but we can still involve Jesus in it by committing it all to Him and consulting Him over decisions to be made. In the evenings when our work is done and the children are in bed we can spend some time with Jesus even if it is late and we are tired. Instead of reading the newspaper or watching television to relax, we can worship Jesus or read more of the Bible, pray or read a challenging spiritual book. I am not saying we should never read the newspaper or watch television but it is very easy to spend too much time on those things. It is a question of priorities. I am not being legalistic – it is a choice. For me, the closer I get to Jesus, the more in love with Him I am, and the less attraction the things of the world have for me. It is not that I cannot do those things – I would just prefer to spend my time with Jesus.

And in between everything we can tell Jesus how much

we love Him. We can tell Him we love Him a thousand times a day and He will not get tired of hearing it! He longs for us to pour out our love to Him – because He loves us, and delights in us! (Proverbs 9:31; Song of Solomon 4:9; 7:10).

Sometimes other religions can be quite challenging. In our work in prisons we visit some Muslims and even in prison they get their prayer mats out, kneel down and pray five times a day facing Mecca. Their first call to prayer is 5 o'clock in the morning! Like the Roman Catholics have Rosary Beads, the Muslims have beads and call on Allah as every bead passes through their fingers. Such devotion! No wonder they believe they will take over the world for Allah! What excuse do we have for neglecting our Lord Jesus Christ?

Proverbs 3:5–6 says,

> 'Trust in the Lord with all your heart, and lean not on your own understanding; in all your ways acknowledge Him, and He shall direct your paths.'

Most Christians, myself included in certain situations, have said many times that they want to do God's will, if only they knew what it was. After the Lord Jesus told me how He wanted me to prepare for the last days, this verse took on a new meaning for me. It did not just mean that He would guide me if I trusted in Him, and it is out of my love relationship with Him that I would know His will and that He would direct my paths. On top of that I felt that Jesus was telling me that **the will of God is not a location or a particular course of action – it is a *relationship* with Him**. If I am in a right relationship with Jesus, loving Him, trusting Him in every way, not only will He make sure I know His will, but also, at that particular moment, I am in the very centre of His will! There is such a security in knowing this; such a joy and liberty, that it sets me free to love and worship Jesus without worrying if I should be doing something else!

Jesus is not just *'the Alpha and the Omega, the Beginning and the End'* (Revelation 1:8), He is also everything in between because He is the Way! (John 14:6). There is no other way I should be going – Jesus Himself is that Way. When I have found Jesus, I have found the Way! Now you may ask, 'the Way where to?' If we look at the Christian life as a journey, Jesus is the Beginning of that journey, the Door (John 10:7–9), to enter on that journey. He is also the End, the End of that journey. If we want to know what the purpose of our life is, the goal, where we should be aiming for, we only have to aim for Jesus. Jesus is our Goal, our End – and He Himself is the only Way to that End. We do not have to seek a ministry or how to serve Jesus. It is true that because we love Him we want to show our love by doing something for Him; we want to please Him. I believe that the best way to show Him we love Him is to spend time with Him, telling Him we love Him and simply resting in Him and enjoying His Presence. Apart from that, it is only as we rest in Jesus that He can speak to us and show us what He wants us to do for Him.

When Martha was complaining that she was doing all the work and her sister Mary was sat at Jesus' feet instead of helping her, Jesus' reply was,

> *'Martha, Martha ... you are worried and upset about many things, but only one thing is needed. Mary has chosen what is better, and it will not be taken away from her.'* (Luke 10:41–42, NIV)

Two meals were being prepared in that house, one by Martha and one by Jesus. Mary was feasting on the meal Jesus had for her. I believe 'sitting at Jesus' feet' pleases Him more than anything else; and it is out of this kind of relationship with Jesus that we can win others to Him. Peter and John were just uneducated fishermen. When they were arrested for preaching the Good News, and brought before the rulers and elders of Jerusalem, they were filled with the Holy Spirit. In Acts 4:13 it says,

> 'Now when they [the rulers and elders] *saw the boldness of Peter and John, and perceived that they were unlearned and ignorant men, they marvelled; and **they took knowledge of them, that they had been with Jesus.'***

We will also find ourselves doing things for Him without having actually planned it! We will find ourselves walking **into** the *'good works which God prepared beforehand'* (Ephesians 2:10).

Jesus wants us not only to love Him, but also to be 'in love' with Him. He wants us to be on fire for Him. In Revelation 3:15–19, Jesus does not mince words in writing to the church in Laodicea:

> 'I know your works, that you are neither cold nor hot. I could wish you were cold or hot. So then, **because you are lukewarm**, and neither cold nor hot, **I will vomit you out of My mouth**. Because you say, "I am rich, have become wealthy, and have need of nothing" – and do not know that you are wretched, miserable, poor, blind, and naked – I counsel you to buy from Me gold refined in the fire.... As many as I love, I rebuke and chasten. Therefore be zealous and repent.'

Can we acknowledge our need?

> 'Blessed are those who hunger and thirst for righteousness, for they shall be filled.' (Matthew 5:6)

> 'He has filled the hungry with good things, and the rich He has sent away empty.' (Luke 1:53)

Verse 20 of that same passage in Revelation says,

> 'Behold, I [Jesus] *stand at the door and knock. If anyone hears My voice and opens the door, I will come in to him and dine with him, and he with Me.'*

This verse is often used to encourage non-Christians to ask Jesus into their hearts, but it is actually talking to people who are already Christians. Jesus wants to come into our lives in a new way. He wants us to open up every area of our lives to Him, so He can have fellowship with us all day, every day – not just on Sundays and perhaps an hour every morning and five minutes before we go to bed at night! Jesus wants us to have a much deeper relationship with Him than we have ever experienced before. Will you open up to Jesus and ask Him to come into **every** area of your life? Will you let Him take control of your life – completely? Will you answer the cry of Jesus' heart and seek a meaningful love relationship with Him?

This intimate love relationship with Jesus is, in my mind, the most important thing for us to concentrate on if we want to be ready for the future. Sometimes, however, there can be things in our lives that stop us from coming into that depth of relationship. I would like to share with you something that hindered my relationship with Jesus for a few years; something that stopped me fully knowing His love for me and stopped me from accepting and responding to that love.

Chapter 3

Dealing With Pain

My husband, Doug, and I came to live in Hong Kong in 1984. After we had been here for a while, a young Chinese man who had gathered some young people around him, asked us to help him establish a church on Bible principles and we were very happy to do so. As the services were all in Cantonese we only understood part of what was happening and the rest through an interpreter – there were several young ladies and the pastor himself who spoke excellent English. Everybody shared in the meetings and we had a very good relationship with the pastor and all the young people. We certainly enjoyed the meetings and had plenty of times of fun with them all. They were like family to us. We loved them and knew that they loved us.

Gradually, however, we noticed a change in the pastor's attitude towards us. He also seemed to be trying to control some of the young people and a few of them left because of it but he refused correction. Then, one day he said that we were not part of the church and he did not want us to come anymore! This came as quite a shock but we felt we had no choice but to stop going. Although we had been in close contact with many of them before this, there was only one of the young people who contacted us and asked us why we had not been to the meetings. She said that the pastor had told everybody that we were too busy to come, giving them the impression that we were not really interested in them, or did not care about them. We did not feel it would be right for us to tell anybody why we had left the church – we did not want to uncover the pastor and we did not want to cause division by encouraging other people to leave. Months later a few others did leave that church and contacted us. It was very sad to hear what was going on but we felt that all we could do was to pray for the pastor – and for protection for the other young people.

All of this was very painful but everytime we thought about it we forgave the pastor, and we continually asked the Lord to bless him in the Name of Jesus.

We started to become more involved in an English-speaking church and the Holy Spirit was beginning to move wonderfully amongst the few that attended the mid-week meetings. Ones and twos were getting baptised in the Holy Spirit, several requested and received deliverance from long-standing problems, and there were one or two remarkable healings. Revival was in the air. We were aware that the devil was not very happy with what was happening so we asked others to pray with and for us accordingly, but we were not prepared for how the devil infiltrated the ranks.

One of the group brought a colleague who said she was interested to know more about Jesus. She certainly asked many questions but in such a way as to undermine us and the teachings of the Bible: 'Surely God doesn't mean "such and such"?' or 'If God loves us then surely "this and that" doesn't matter?' She seemed to hold many New Age ideas.

This lady was quite rich and going through some marriage problems and several people felt sorry for her and she soon won them over to her way of thinking. She and one or two of the others started complaining about us among themselves and then to the minister who did not usually come to the mid-week meetings. One evening we arrived at the meeting a few minutes late and were surprised to see the minister there. We greeted him (we had always had a good relationship with him and had 'agreed to differ' over certain points of doctrine we did not see eye to eye on), and asked him to what we owed the pleasure of his company. He seemed rather cool and said he wanted to see what was going on in the meetings. We had a sinking feeling in our stomachs and began to feel very uncomfortable. There was definitely an 'atmosphere' as we looked around the room. Most of the people were looking at their shoes! Noticeably absent was this particular lady. Two other ladies, with whom we felt spiritually one and who had always contributed very positively to the meetings, were away on holiday.

Slowly it all came out. Although we were not leading the meetings and everybody participated, many times people asked us questions and we were just answering them from the Bible. However, the answers were not always what they wanted to hear. The final straw had been when somebody wanted to bring some homosexuals to the church and asked us what we thought about it. We had said that they would certainly be welcome in the meetings, but if it was possible we would also try to show them that, in God's eyes, what they were doing was not right and help them to get free of it. Those who thought we were wrong had gone to the minister to complain. Now we found that he held to the view that homosexuality was not a sin but just a different life-style and he saw no reason why practising homosexuals could not be good Christians or even be ministers in the Church. When we pointed out what the Bible said in Romans 1:20–32 (NIV) and in Leviticus 18:22; 20:13 against homosexuality, the minister said he did not believe the Old Testament or Paul's writings, only the Gospels!

We looked around the room for some support from the rest of the group. Nobody said a word. They were too busy examining the floor between their feet or the speck of dirt under their finger nails! With horror we realised we were on our own. Not one person came to our defence – or the Bible's defence! Didn't they believe it anymore? After an uneasy silence one or two started complaining about other things we had done or said – things which had obviously convicted them, for example, being *'unequally yoked together with unbelievers'* (2 Corinthians 6:14).

I was in such shock that I could not stop the tears pouring down my cheeks. These were our friends; people we had shared with and ministered to and we loved them. We thought they had loved us too. Now they were not only rejecting us but they were rejecting Jesus. How could they do that after all He had done for them?

We drove home in stunned silence. Over a cup of tea Doug and I talked about what had happened. We forgave them all – the minister, the people in the group, the lady who we realised had started the unrest, and we asked God to bless each one in Jesus' Name. Proverbs 4:23 says, *'Keep your heart with all diligence, for out of it spring the issues of life,'* so we knew it was important to keep our hearts free from any bitterness or resentment. In the Name of Jesus we declared our love for them. Though we were also sorely tempted to say, 'Well, we're not going there again!' we knew we must not make that kind of decision based on our emotions. We asked the Lord Jesus, our *'Friend who sticks closer than a brother'* (Proverbs 18:24), what He wanted us to do.

The following day there were several verses in our Bible readings that stood out to us including,

> *'He who is not with Me is against Me, and he who does not gather with Me scatters abroad,'*   (Matthew 12:30)

and,

> *'Let them return to you, but you must not return to them ... they will fight against you, but they shall not prevail against you ...'*   (Jeremiah 15:19–21)

After much prayer and soul-searching that we were not making this decision because we felt hurt and rejected, but because we felt it was what the Lord was saying to us, we decided we could not possibly continue to attend the mid-week meetings. If the people did not accept the Bible as God's Word then there was no common ground for fellowship with them. We also did not feel we could carry on teaching the Sunday School. That was an even more difficult decision because we really loved those children. Amongst other things we did not feel it was right for us to knowingly take them each week to the altar rail for hands to be laid on them and to be blessed by a man who so openly accepted and approved of homosexuality in the church.

There were several other incidents around that time that compounded the hurt and rejection I was feeling. A Christian young man we knew wrote over sixty pages of accusations against us, mainly concerning the gifts of the Holy Spirit, and gave it to other pastors. A Christian lady who used to live with us, to whom we had been quite close, and whom we had helped a lot, even to furnish her own apartment in a different area, was hurt because another brother refused to date her. She blamed us and rang us up at 1 pm on Christmas Day and, amidst a tirade of accusations, told us we were deceived and how dare we do and say some of the things we supposedly had done and said. She so blackened our names, and that of this brother, that we were not welcome in several other churches and the husband of a good friend forbade me to enter his home or see his wife again. There is a saying that 'hell has no fury like a woman scorned'!

All these things and other incidents before and after, had left me feeling very bruised. I did not want to get close to anybody in case they hurt me. I was careful not to let a spirit of rejection come in – I had been delivered of that years earlier and I did not want it again. I was also careful to continue forgiving all these people every time they came to my thoughts. At first it had been difficult. It was an act of my will, not a feeling, but I knew I must forgive as Jesus had forgiven me. As time passed and we got involved with other things and other people, I pushed these events to the back of my memory and I hardly thought about them anymore.

Months later, however, a good friend, Chris, rang me up, asking me how I was. I said I was fine but she insisted, 'No. How are you really?'

'I'm fine,' I repeated.

'Why are you in such pain, then?'

That shocked me; 'I'm OK. There's nothing wrong with me.'

But unexplainably I felt the tears welling up. 'I'm alright,' I continued to insist, but I knew she had touched something deep down inside me.

Over the next few months Chris helped me to deal with the pain that I had buried and had built up inside. Yes, I had truly forgiven all the people who had hurt me, directly or indirectly, knowingly or unknowingly. I felt no bitterness or resentment towards them – but there was still all the pain that I had tried to ignore by pushing it deeper and deeper down inside.

At first it was difficult to talk about the things that had happened. Doug and I had not spoken to other people about most of those situations. How could we without uncovering our brothers and sisters? Chris did not pry, or insist that I tell her, but it seemed that whenever we got together to pray I would just start to cry and cry – the pain was so great. It was as though Jesus Himself was deliberately stirring it up so I could not ignore it any longer. One by one I talked about these events. Each time I seemed to experience **all** the hurt and pain that had accumulated, not just that which I had felt from each individual incident when it was actually happening – and it hurt so much that I could hardly speak. It came to the point that I almost dreaded those times of prayer! I sometimes wondered if it was worth it. Couldn't I just leave things the way they were? Couldn't the pain stay buried like it was previously? I had been coping alright before – well, sort of! But Jesus was not letting me bury it.

He loved me so much that He wanted to set me free from it, all of it. By faith I had to accept that He knew what He was doing, and *'He has done all things well'* (Mark 7:37).

Week by week Jesus dealt with the pain and slowly a pattern emerged; the steps Jesus wanted me to take to get free of the pain. I list them here, not as a fixed way it has got to be done (the Lord is a Creator and has many ways to deal with our problems, tailored to meet each individual's need), but as a guideline for others who may be in great pain as I was. You may find it beneficial to talk to somebody you can trust spiritually, and who can help you deal with your pain like I did, but I believe it can also be done by yourself if necessary. Here are the steps I took:

1. Recognise the problem and be willing to forgive myself and the other person.
2. Acknowledge who caused the damage, i.e. myself or another person.
3. If it is myself, ask Jesus to forgive me.
4. Renounce the pain and release it to Jesus.
5. In the Name of Jesus, command Satan to remove the hold he has over the other person because of the sin they have committed. *'Whatsoever you bind on earth* [having been bound in heaven] *will be bound..., and whatsoever you loose on earth* [having been loosed in heaven] *will be loosed...'* (Matthew 18:18, original translation).
6. Release the person to the Holy Spirit to convict and deal with.
7. Receive the love of Jesus and His comfort.
8. Enter into the freedom and healing power of Jesus – by faith.

It was steps 4, 7 and 8 which were particularly necessary for me. I had previously forgiven the other people and had frequently prayed for them but now I had to renounce and release the pain to Jesus. He had already taken that pain on Himself on the Cross:

'Surely He has borne our griefs, and carried our sorrows.'
(Isaiah 53:4)

But I had to **see** that He had taken it, just as years before, when I had first come to know Jesus as my Messiah, I had seen that He had taken my sins on Himself and received the punishment I deserved:

'Who His own self bare our sins in His own body on the Tree, that we, being dead to sins, should live unto righteousness...'
(2 Peter 2:24)

In the past I had also seen that

'[Jesus] *'Himself took our infirmities And bore our sicknesses.'*
(Matthew 8:17)

As I had had to mix those scriptures with faith, so I had to mix this with faith when I released the pain to Jesus.

Then, again by faith, I had to consciously **receive** the love and comfort that Jesus wanted me to have. The Holy Spirit, the Spirit of Jesus Himself, is the Comforter (John 14:16, 26). During these weeks of dealing with the pain, and for some time afterwards, as I spent time with Jesus I would say 'I **receive** Your love. I receive Your comfort.' From a book I read at that time, *Comfort For The Wounded Spirit* by Frank and Ida Mae Hammond (New Wine Press), I realised that I had been **refusing** the Lord's comfort, like Jacob when he thought his favourite son, Joseph, had been killed by a wild animal:

*'All his sons and his daughters arose to comfort him; but he **refused to be comforted**, and he said, "For I shall go down into the grave to my son mourning."'*
(Genesis 37:35)

[It is an interesting thought that if Jacob had reached out to the Lord in his grief and pain, the Lord could have revealed to him that Joseph was not dead!]

Gradually I began to feel Jesus' love and His comfort,

'Who comforts us in all our tribulation, that we may be able to comfort those who are in any trouble, with the comfort with which we ourselves are comforted by God.'

(2 Corinthians 1:4)

Finally, I had to take the step of entering into freedom.

'It is for freedom that Christ has set us free.'

(Galatians 5:1, NIV)

At the time it was **only** by faith. I did not immediately **feel** any lifting of the pain; I just had to believe it, and slowly, gradually, it disappeared. It was like when somebody has an operation to remove some painful, diseased tissue. After the anaesthetic has worn off there is still a lot of pain but it gradually eases and eventually stops altogether as the incision and the inner tissue heals and the surface scar fades. Now, several years later, I can testify that all that pain has completely gone. I have not even felt a twinge of it as I have been writing about those painful episodes – just a joy and a heart full of gratitude to Jesus for what He has done! Hallelujah!

This is not to say that no more difficult and hurtful things have happened. The devil is not called the accuser of the brethren for nothing (Revelation 12:10), and he is very clever at causing misunderstandings! But Jesus has shown me what to do with the pain and I do not need to harden my heart so I do not feel anything. As there is now no backlog of pain for new pain to build on, things do not hurt so much anyway – and what little pain there may be, I can immediately give it to Jesus and see Him bear it for me on the Cross. Thank You, Jesus!

Is there pain in your life? You do not have to live with it any longer. Release it to Jesus. Let Him take it. By faith believe that He has taken it and then enter into the freedom that He purchased for you on the Cross, and thank Him for it.

'For this purpose the Son of God was manifested, that He might destroy the works of the devil.' (1 John 3:8)

Only as the pain was dealt with in my life was I free to come into a deeper, more meaningful relationship with Jesus. But how could I go about it?

Chapter 4

Falling in Love

Because of the pain in my life, for two or three years that deep fellowship with Jesus had been missing. Yes, I still loved Him, prayed and read my Bible every day, and talked to others about Him at every opportunity – but that deep, intimate love relationship had grown cold.

In the early part of 1995 I met a lady who had only known Jesus for a few months but obviously had that love relationship with Him. I became even more aware of my lack. She would talk naturally of Jesus telling her this or showing her that and I thought, 'But He doesn't speak to **me** like that! He used to, but not any more.' The more I observed this lady and her hunger to know more of Jesus, the more dissatisfied I was with my own relationship with Him and I began to cry out for more. One passage of Scripture that has always challenged me is Revelation 2:1–7, especially verses 4 and 5, where Jesus is writing to the church at Ephesus:

> *'Nevertheless I have this against you, that you have left your first love. Remember therefore from where you have fallen; repent and do the first works, or else I will come to you quickly and remove your lampstand from its place – unless you repent.'*

I read it again, and I was convicted again. I had to confess that I had left my first love. That is what this lady had – her first love! Her initial love and zeal for Jesus who loved her so much that He died for her! When some people meet a new Christian with all their love and zeal, I have heard them say, 'Oh, it will soon wear off.' But Jesus does not want it to wear off – and it does not need to, even when trials and testings come along, otherwise He

41

would not have told the church at Ephesus to repent of it wearing off!

During the previous few years whenever I had read this passage I had had to admit that I had left my first love and I would ask the Lord to forgive me. I would tell Jesus that I wanted that first love back again. But I did not know **how** to get it back! This time, as I asked the Lord Jesus to forgive me, I suddenly noticed the words *'do the first works'* as though I had never seen them before. 'The first works! What are those first works, Lord? Show me what they are so I can do them again.'

I thought back to when I first met Jesus more than twenty-five years ago. Apart from avidly reading the Bible and memorising scriptures, I would talk to Jesus almost all the time. Many times, too, I would just sit quietly and tell Jesus how much I loved Him. As I relaxed I could feel His arms of love around me. Joy and peace flooded my soul. The busier I was, the more I did it – and the more I needed to do it! Song of Solomon 1:7 says,

> *'Tell me, O You whom I love,*
> *Where You feed Your flock,*
> *Where You make it rest at noon . . . ?'*

Noon is the hottest part of the day. The time I most need to rest and relax in Jesus, even if it is only for a few minutes, is during the heat of the day, in the midst of the battles. The time I most need to relax is when I am busy and, naturally speaking, do not have time to relax! I realised I had been **too** busy. Everybody in Hong Kong is busy. Ask somebody how they are and the reply is nearly always 'Busy!' It is almost like there must be something wrong with you if you are **not** busy! But this was not right. Just because other people were influenced by this busy spirit did not mean I had to let it affect me. I had to ask Jesus to forgive me for getting caught up with that busyness. I had not **made** time to rest and tell Jesus how much I loved Him. I had forgotten how important it was.

From then on I made every effort to spend time alone with Jesus, apart from my normal quiet times in the mornings when I read the Bible and prayed. I found a lovely spot by the river only five minutes walk from home, and would sit there loving Jesus and listening to worship tapes on my walkman, for half an hour or so most days. I had lots of work to do at my desk, even urgent things, but I decided to put Jesus first. I wanted that 'first love' back again so I had to make a deliberate choice to do what was important, not what was urgent!

To begin with I did not **feel** anything – except an emptiness inside. Jesus seemed so far away. Where was He? Why didn't He speak to me anymore? Most of the time I just cried when I was down by the river. And when I heard others talking about Jesus I would cry too. I wondered what was wrong with me.

At about that time a friend gave me a tape by Kevin Prosch. As I was listening to it for the first time, late one night, I heard the words of one of the songs: 'I've cried out for more; there has to be more....' My ears pricked up. Inwardly I cried out, '**Yes!** Lord – I **have** cried out for more!' The tears started to flow uncontrollably as it continued:

> '... place in my heart, a passion for You,
> Like none that I've ever had.
> My eyes fill with longing for Your words of life;
> I'm hungry for all that You have.
> And don't let my mind deceive my heart;
> Give me the strength to press in.
> Should I build an altar and stay here?
> And grow old and say I'm content
> When will we meet again?
> I must have more; I know there is more;
> There has to be more!
> How can I be satisfied,
> Unless You come near and stay by my side?

Call me Your friend; count me in for life.
Oh how can I be satisfied...?'

(*How Can I Be Satisfied* by Kevin Prosch
– 7th Time Music)

Every word echoed the longing in my heart. I **had** cried out for more. How could I be satisfied like I was? I yearned to meet with Jesus again, in a deeper way. I needed a fresh revelation of His love. Others might be content to drift along in their spiritual life but I was hungry and I knew there was more. There **had** to be more!

I played this song over and over again, weeping continually and pleading with Jesus to 'place in my heart a **passion** for Him, like none that I've ever had!' Over the next days and weeks the longing in my heart for Jesus only increased. He seemed further away than ever. 'Oh, Jesus! When will we meet again?'

I went to a ladies' two-day retreat and spent quite a bit of the time still crying out to Jesus. On the last day the speaker had personal prophecies for each of the ladies. She gave me Song of Solomon 8:5,

> *'Who is this coming up from the wilderness,*
> *Leaning upon her beloved?'*

She did not know anything about me but said that I had been going through a dry, desert experience but through it, I was learning to lean on my Beloved and she urged me to lean even more. This was a great encouragement to me and I had renewed confidence that Jesus was with me, although I could not feel Him. Of course, He had never left me. My head knew that anyway, because the Bible told me so in Hebrews 13:5, *'I will never leave you nor forsake you.'* And after all, *'we walk by faith and not by sight* [or by feelings]' (2 Corinthians 5:7). I read somewhere recently about a minister who was trying to encourage an old Christian lady who was dying. He read to her Jesus' words from Matthew 28:20, *'Lo, I am with you always,'* saying what a wonderful promise that was. The lady replied, 'Sir. That isn't a promise – it's a fact!' Hallelujah!

Very soon after this we were invited for the first time to go to the Philippines to speak at a Christian convention. I've talked more about this in a later chapter but now I'll just say that this was a time of walking by faith in a deeper way than I had ever experienced previously. Jesus had been very real to me and had demonstrated His love and faithfulness in so many ways. When we returned to Hong Kong I was very busy because the work on my desk had piled up while we were away and I had many letters to write and lots of books to mail to those around the world who had requested them. Even so I tried to spend as much time as possible worshipping Jesus. His love was becoming more real to me again. We then made another trip to the Philippines where I continually spoke about spending time with Jesus, telling Him we love Him, and developing that love relationship with Him.

But inside, I still knew there was more. I knew that my own relationship with Jesus was not deep enough. I cried out for a deeper **revelation** of His love. I listened again and again to Kevin Prosch's song – and again and again I cried out for more, for Jesus to increase in my heart a passion for Him.

At last it came. I suddenly realised it was **Jesus! He** was all I needed! I did not have to look for anything beyond Jesus. In fact, I did not have to look for Jesus – He was with me all the time but I needed a **revelation** of it. [I pray that also *'the God of our Lord Jesus Christ, the Father of glory, may give to you the spirit of wisdom and revelation in the knowledge of Him'* (Ephesians 1:17).] And He was not just with me, He was living **in** me! I did not need to strive to please God, to discover His will, or to be something I wasn't. All He wanted me to do was to relax and enjoy Him! I can hardly describe the joy that flooded my soul as I was overwhelmed with His love and His Presence. I found myself repeating over and over, 'I love You, Jesus. I love You, Jesus! I love You, Jesus!'

The Lord Jesus Christ Himself is **love**. Jesus is *'the Way, the Truth and the Life'* (John 14:6). I suddenly realised I did not need any thing or any experience outside of Jesus! Jesus is All in all! He is *'the Author and Finisher...'* (Hebrews 12:2). I was *'complete in Him'* (Colossians 2:10).

And that is still my experience, day after day, when things are going right or when everything is contrary to what I would want. My love relationship with Jesus is not dependent on outward circumstances or my feelings. Jesus is still *'the same yesterday, and today, and forever'* (Hebrews 13:8). The fact that He is with me and lives within me and loves me, I have to mix with faith! It is different, of course, if I start to worry about something or let any sin, no matter how small, hide His precious face from me. The moment I lose my peace or come out of a rest, which means I am not trusting Him in that particular situation, I must confess my sin; and Jesus is *'faithful and just to forgive us our sins, and to cleanse is from all unrighteousness'* (1 John 1:9). Then immediately my heart is filled with joy again and all I want to do is worship my wonderful, wonderful Jesus, the Lover of my soul.

Brother, sister – are you 'complete in Him'? I would encourage you, even challenge you, to spend extra time with Jesus, apart from your usual time of prayer and Bible reading. Be alone with Jesus and tell Him how much you love Him, even if it is only a few minutes each day, perhaps during your lunch break. If you do not feel that love, ask Jesus to 'place in your heart a passion' for Him. Cry out to Him – and keep on crying out to Him, for a revelation of His love, for a revelation of Himself. Do not give up. 'Don't let your mind deceive your heart... **Press in.**' For me it took about two years from when I first began to set apart time each day to seek Jesus, and to worship Him. For you it may only be a few days or weeks, or maybe it will be a longer time, but don't give up. You **will** find Jesus when you search for Him with all your heart (Jeremiah 29:13). Be determined and I know Jesus will answer the longing of your heart. He **will** reveal Himself to you in a fresh and deeper way. Not only does Jesus tell us to repent if we have lost our first love for Him but also I cannot emphasise too much that without this love relationship with Him, we may not be able to cope with the trials and tribulations of these last days.

Every good relationship needs to be worked at. If we want to have a good relationship with our husbands or wives, we must work at it. If we want to have a good relationship with our family members or friends, we must work at it. If we want to have a good relationship with Jesus we must work at it. And once we have achieved a good relationship we must continue to work at it or else it will die. I cannot say I've arrived at a particular spiritual level and therefore I don't need to seek Jesus any more. Like the Apostle Paul I say,

> 'Not that I have already attained, or am already perfected; but I **press on**, that I may lay hold of that for which Christ Jesus has also laid hold of me.'
>
> (Philippians 3:12)

I do not want to stay where I am now; I want to continue to develop my relationship with Jesus. In fact, I think we can compare our spiritual life with trying to walk up an escalator that is coming down – if we stop walking we will go down; we have to continue walking to even stay where we are! If we don't want to progress in our spiritual life and we stop any spiritual activity, like going to church, praying or reading the Bible, we will gradually go down and down, getting spiritually weaker and weaker. We have to make a determined effort to go on with Jesus, seeking Him and continually crying out for a fresh revelation of Him and a deeper relationship with Him.

We need to be spiritually strong if we are going to be able to stand during the difficulties and persecution that the end times may bring.

Once we have come into a deep, intimate love relationship with Jesus, how then can we keep it alive; how can we maintain it?

PART TWO

Maintaining Our Relationship

Chapter 5

Bible Reading

I have met many Christians who have not grown very much since they first got saved because they only read their Bible on a Sunday, or perhaps just a few verses each day. That is what I would call a starvation diet! To grow and to maintain a strong and healthy Christian life we need more than just a few mouthfuls of spiritual food. I would even say that only reading one chapter a day is not enough. Most of us eat three meals a day of natural food and even if we are very busy we make sure we have time to eat. In fact, for most people their whole day revolves around mealtimes! I'm not saying this is wrong but if we lay so much importance on our natural food, shouldn't we also lay at least equal importance on our spiritual food? Job even said,

> *'I have treasured the words of His mouth **more** than my necessary food.'* (Job 23:12)

If we make sure we have time to eat, then we should make sure we have time to read the Bible. It does not have to be three times a day, though that is good, but we should plan our day in such a way that we have time to read three or four chapters each day.

I am very grateful to Patty, the lady who led me to the Lord many years ago, and encouraged me to spend time at the beginning of each day in Bible reading and prayer. That was the beginning of a habit that is still with me, and it was a habit well worth cultivating. In those days I started work at 7 am so it meant getting up at 5.30 am if I wanted an hour with Jesus. A few years later, when I was living and working on a kibbutz in Israel, I started work at 6 am so I had to get up at 4.30 am. It also meant I had to go to bed a lot earlier than all the other young people who were talking and partying sometimes until midnight. Our wonderful Lord Jesus gave me the ability and grace to sleep through the noise, even though the walls were only made of plywood, and then woke me up each morning exactly on time. I couldn't use an alarm-clock because it would have woken up my room-mates. For the same reason I had to find some other place to meet with Jesus because it was still dark and I didn't want to put the light on. But without those times with Jesus at the beginning of the day, I don't know if I would have had the ability and grace to cope with the rest of the day!

I would like to say a word here to mothers with very young children. I do know that it is not easy for you to find time to be alone with Jesus because the children demand your attention all the time they are awake. Here in Hong Kong most of the children, even 3 or 4 year-olds, don't go to bed until 10 or 11 pm. Not only is this not good for the children (most of them are falling asleep in class or on the bus to and from school), but it is also not good for the parents because they have no time to be alone together and the friendship they had before they were married soon disappears. In England and probably in some other western countries, young children are usually in bed by 7 or 8 pm. This means the parents can, if they choose, have time together and also they can have time to be alone with Jesus. You will say that by that time you are so tired that you fall asleep every time you try to read the Bible or pray. If that is the case, try going to bed early instead of watching television, and then you will be able to get up earlier, before the children wake up. Even a little bit of time alone with Jesus, worshipping, praying, reading the Bible is better than none for those times when more is impossible. Our wonderful Lord Jesus knows our hearts and our desire to be with Him. If the children do wake up and disturb you then explain to them that this is your time to be with Jesus and they can

51

play quietly in their bedroom until you tell them it is time to get up. A little bit of discipline and training will do them the world of good. And remember, parents should be the ones who run the home and make the decisions, not the children!

A few years ago my husband and I were visiting some friends in Eilat, Israel. We were not actually staying with our friends but spent most afternoons and evenings with them. After a few days we noticed that the wife disappeared every evening at about 8.30 pm. She did not say anything; she just quietly got up and went out of the room. At first we had thought she was going to the bathroom or to check up on their four young children who had gone to bed a while earlier. Later we realised she had not come back into the living room where Doug and I were fellowshipping with her husband and sometimes two or three other Christians. We asked her husband where she was and he told us she had gone to bed because she would get up every morning at about 4.30 am to spend time alone with Jesus before the children woke up.

This lady was not being rude; in no way did we feel she was ignoring us guests. We had been with her during the day and I had had wonderful fellowship with her while we prepared the evening meal together. But she put time alone with Jesus as being more important than time spent in fellowship with friends. She denied herself. In Luke 9:23 Jesus says,

> 'If anyone desires to come after Me, let him deny himself, and take up his cross daily, and follow Me.'

Many of us will say we want to follow Jesus, but are we willing to deny ourselves? Are we willing to voluntarily take up our cross each day? It is not forced upon us; it is something we can choose to take up or not. Somebody once described taking up the cross as being when the will of God **crosses** my will; when His will goes contrary to what I want. The letter 'I' (which represents me, myself, my ego) when it is crossed out, when it has a line through it, it forms a Cross! When we voluntarily do something because we know it is what Jesus wants us to do, even though it may not be what we ourselves would choose, but purely because we love Jesus and want to please Him – that is denying ourselves; that is taking up our cross. That is a sacrifice that is well-pleasing to the Lord; a sweet fragrance to Him.

Now some may say they read the Bible but it is dry and they don't know if they are reading the right part. Anybody who has tried to read the Bible from beginning to end will agree that it is hard going in some parts of Leviticus and Numbers, and then in some of the prophets too! A daily Bible-reading plan (see Appendix) which includes reading different parts of the Bible each day, is very useful: we know where we should read every day and the variety makes it more interesting. It is also a good discipline though it should never become a bondage. We should read the Bible because we love Jesus and because we want to know what He is saying to us each day. If we still find it difficult to read the Bible we can ask Jesus to give us a hunger for His Word. If there is no change immediately don't give up – keep on asking and keep on reading!

Reading the Bible is important for several reasons. Apart from it being our spiritual food and making us strong and healthy, it is God's Word and it shows us more about Him and His ways, and reveals to us His thoughts and therefore helps us get to know Him. When we buy a new gadget or some electrical appliance we always receive an instruction manual with it so we know how to use it. The Bible is our instruction manual, the Maker's Handbook on how to live the life He has given to us! The more we read His Word, asking the Lord Jesus to reveal Himself to us as we read, the more we will get to know Him and how to live His life in this world.

It is also one of the chief ways the Lord speaks to us; to encourage us, comfort us, show us when we are wrong and also to show us what to do or where to go. The Apostle Paul said,

> 'All Scripture is given by inspiration of God, and is profitable for doctrine, for reproof, for correction, for instruction in righteousness, that the man [or woman or child] of God may be complete, thoroughly equipped for every good work.' (2 Timothy 3:16–17)

Later in the book I will relate some different ways Jesus has spoken to me through His Word.

Not only is God's Word our spiritual food, it is also like water which washes and cleanses us within from any impurities:

> 'Christ also loved the church and gave Himself for her, that He might sanctify and cleanse her with the washing of water **by the word**, that He might present her to Himself a glorious church, not having spot or wrinkle or any such thing, but that she should be holy and without blemish.' (Ephesians 5:26)

We might not see the importance of this for us now but we will when Jesus returns for His Bride – whenever that may be in relation to the Tribulation. Not everybody will be called to the marriage supper of the Lamb, otherwise the angels would not have told the Apostle John on the island of Patmos,

> 'Write: "Blessed are those who are called to the marriage supper of the Lamb!"' (Revelation 19:9)

In verse 7 of the same chapter it says,

> 'The wedding of the Lamb has come, and His bride has made herself ready' (NIV)

Are we ready for the marriage supper of the Lamb? Will we be among the blessed who are called to that marriage supper? Jesus, *'the Lamb of God who takes away the sin of the world,'* (John 1:29) is coming for the Church, *'prepared as a bride adorned for her husband'* (Revelation 21:2), *'holy and without blame before Him'* (Ephesians 1:4). We will talk more about being holy later.

Another reason for reading the Bible is to renew our minds. Romans 12:2 says,

> *'Do not be conformed to this world, but be transformed by the renewing of your mind, that you may prove what is that good and acceptable and perfect will of God.'*

Ephesians 4:23 also says we should be *'renewed in the spirit of* [our] *mind.'*

When I first got saved somebody told me that our minds are like a tape recording – everything that has happened to us and everything we have read, heard or learnt, is stored up in our minds. Of course, some of this is good but a great deal of it colours how we think and react and that is not always so good.

> *'If anyone is in Christ, he is a new creation; old things have passed away; behold, all things have become new.'*
> (2 Corinthians 5:17)

A new creation must have a new mind and a new way of thinking and reacting – God's way.

> *'Because as He is, so are we in this world.'*
> (1 John 4:17b)

And

> *'He who says he abides in Him ought himself also to walk just as He walked.'* (1 John 2:6)

The best way of removing something off a tape is by recording over it. We remove something off the recording of our minds by recording over them and feeding them with spiritual things, especially the Word of God.

If we spend a lot of time with somebody we get to know

them and what they will do or how they will think in certain situations, and we become like them in many ways. Doug and I have spent so much time together that we know each other very well and we have become more like each other. We often think the same and sometimes we both say the same thing at exactly the same time, in unison! The more time we spend with Jesus, reading His Word, the more our minds will be renewed and we become more like Him, and conformed to His image. We can get to know Jesus so well and know exactly how He thinks, according to His Word, that *'we have the mind of Christ,'* (1 Corinthians 2:16b). This does take time – it does not happen overnight but there is usually a noticeable difference in somebody almost immediately they ask Jesus to become Lord of their lives and they start reading His Word. I have met some people that still think and react like the 'natural man' and not spiritually, although they have been Christians for quite a while. Their minds have not been renewed and very often this is because they have not been reading the Bible very much – or else they spend too much time reading secular books or watching television which are not necessarily bad things in themselves but do not help us to grow spiritually. An important thing to remember is that **we become like the people we spend time with, so we need to spend time with the people we want to become like**. If we want to become like Jesus we must spend a lot of time with Him. If we spend a lot of time with non-Christians we will be like them. Of course we need to spend **some** time with non-Christians, especially our families, because that is how we will win them to Christ, but if possible we should make sure that most of our time is with Jesus and other Christians. If you live in an area where there are no other Christians and no churches, you can still spend your time with Jesus and He will become your closest Friend.

Memorising Scripture is also very important. I know it is not easy for most of us but there are several reasons why we should try to do it. The first reason is because the Lord Jesus often wants to speak to us in our thoughts and if we have memorised Scripture then He can remind us of it whenever it is necessary, in the midst of any situation, without us actually having our Bibles in front of us. In John 14:26 Jesus says,

> 'The Helper, the Holy Spirit, whom the Father will send in My Name, He will teach you all things, and **bring to your remembrance all things that I said to you.**'

This may be for our own personal edification, comfort or encouragement when we are in a difficult situation and it can also stop us from doing the wrong thing. King David said,

> 'Your word have I hidden in my heart,
> That I might not sin against You.'   (Psalm 119:11)

The Word will keep us from sin but sin will keep us from the Word!

Knowing the Bible is also very useful when we are talking to other people about Jesus. We can speak the verses to them in a natural sort of way which does not sound too 'preachy' or, if we have memorised the reference, we can find the verses quickly in the Bible and let them read it for themselves. When we are talking to people about Jesus, we may think that our words are not having any effect but if we use Scripture, we know that it is

> '... living and powerful, and sharper than any two-edged sword, piercing even to the division of soul and spirit, and of joints and marrow, and is a discerner of the thoughts and intents of the heart.'   (Hebrews 4:12)

In Isaiah 55:11 the Lord also says,

> 'My word ... shall not return to Me void, but it shall accomplish what I please, and it shall prosper in the thing for which I sent it.'

A few months after I came to know the Lord Jesus I was in a short-term Bible School in Germany. Every day except Sunday we had to memorise a Bible verse and every day we were tested on all the previous verses we had learnt. At the end of six weeks I knew thirty-six scriptures which I still remember today. It wasn't always easy but I am very grateful that I had to do it. If it is difficult for you to memorise Scripture you will find it very helpful to do it with another person. Look for somebody, your spouse, a friend or somebody in the church, who also wants to learn, and do it together, testing each other every day. Don't try to do too much at once and choose verses that are meaningful to you. When we have learnt a verse we need to keep revising it every few days or we will soon forget it, and the more we use the scripture, the more it will become a part of us.

Perhaps the most important reason for memorising Scripture is because in the last days there may come a time when we don't have a Bible! At this time Christians in most countries have their own Bible but this may not continue. There are already some places where many thousands of Christians do not have a Bible because when Islam or Communism takes over a country one of the first things that happens is that Bibles are confiscated and burnt. Sometimes there is just one Bible between hundreds of people so they each have one page and when they have read that and memorised it, they exchange it with somebody for another page. If somebody is imprisoned for their faith they will probably not be able to have a Bible, but if they have God's Word hidden in their hearts it will not matter so much. The Holy Spirit will be able to bring back to their remembrance the scriptures they have previously memorised, to encourage them and strengthen them. I cannot think of an occasion when we will more need the Bible than when we are not allowed to have one! We must not take it for granted now, when things are easy, but treasure it and hide it in our hearts. I really hope this will not happen to you or I but if it does, then we need to be prepared. How will we be able to stand strong in Jesus if we do not have His Word in our hearts? Don't say it will never happen to you – all of us need to be prepared. If it does not happen we still have not lost anything by memorising the Scriptures, but gained immeasurably by reading it over and over and learning God's Word until it becomes part of us; until, in fact, the Word becomes flesh in us (John 1:14a).

Chapter 6

Praying

Praying is talking with Jesus. There are different types of prayer like spiritual warfare and intercession, which are very important, but there are many wonderful books written about these so I would like to concentrate on the simpler ways of talking to Jesus which we can all do.

For a healthy emotional life we need love and companionship. Babies normally get this from their parents, brothers and sisters. Later, as children grow, they also need friends who accept them and from whom they can learn. As Christians, we also need the right kind of companionship. In the end times we may find we are in situations where there are no other Christians around us, especially if we are imprisoned for our faith like I already mentioned. Our very best Friend for all of us should be Jesus. We can talk to Him wherever we are, anytime day or night, about anything. We do not have to close our eyes or kneel to pray, or hold our hands together, or adopt any other particular posture, though there are times when it is helpful to do so. We only close our eyes so we can concentrate and not be distracted by people or things around us. I find it helpful to stay in my bedroom to pray because then I am not distracted by the things in my kitchen that need to be done. I also love to walk as I pray and pray as I walk (with my eyes open, of course!). But we need to cultivate the habit of talking to Jesus all the time and about everything; that is what He wants because that is why He created us – to have fellowship with Him (1 Corinthians 1:9). This will help us to develop a meaningful love relationship with Him.

Once we have a good relationship with somebody we have to maintain it. My husband and I have a very good relationship but if I stopped talking to him or never spent any time with him and was always out with my friends, he would certainly think I did not love him anymore and our relationship would die. To keep our relationship alive and fresh we continually tell each other 'I love you' and spend as much time with each other as possible, talking about the things that have happened during the day, and how we feel. We have to continually **work** at our relationship. In the same way we need to work at our relationship with Jesus, by spending time with Him – not just for an hour or two on a Sunday morning, or even half an hour each day. How would it be if I only spent half an hour with my husband and then ignored him the rest of the day?

Jesus is the Lover of our souls and longs for us to spend time with Him, **communing** with Him. Communion with Jesus is communicating with Him. My dictionary defines to 'commune' as to 'feel at one with; be in close touch with; talk with in an intimate way.' Prayer is communion with Jesus which is a two-way communication. In any meaningful relationship both partners talk and commune with each other. If we know somebody who always does all the talking and never gives us time to say anything it is very frustrating, isn't it? We don't particularly want to be with them because it is only a one-sided relationship. Listening is an important part of communication. In the same way, listening to Jesus and what He wants to say to us is just as important, if not more important, than us talking to Him. So prayer is not just talking to Him, telling Him what we want or how we feel, but it is also listening to Jesus talking to us. If I ask Him a question I must wait for an answer. Sometimes I have found myself asking Doug a question and then carrying on talking, not giving him an opportunity to reply. Sometimes I've asked a question and then been so busy with my own thoughts that I don't hear the reply and I have to ask him again. I wonder how many times

I've asked Jesus a question and not waited for the answer? If somebody asks us a question and then doesn't bother to listen to the answer we think how rude they are! 'Forgive me, Lord Jesus, for the many times I've done that with You.'

Because Jesus is interested in every detail of our lives, He **wants** us to involve Him in all that we do. Most of us, perhaps, ask Him about big decisions we need to make, like whom to marry, which house to buy or what job to take. But I feel that Jesus wants us to ask Him about the smaller things too: 'What should I cook for dinner today?' 'What should I wear for this appointment?' 'Should I hang the washing outside or is it going to rain?' Perhaps you think these things are far too trivial to 'bother' the Creator of the Universe about – He's too busy with more important matters. But Jesus is *'a Friend who sticks closer than a brother'* (Proverbs 18:24), and He is our *'Wonderful Counsellor'* (Isaiah 9:6).

You may wonder how it is possible to talk to Jesus all day long. First of all, we do not have to be actually talking to somebody to be in communion with them. When we love somebody we just enjoy being with them and don't always feel the need to be talking all the time. There is a sort of silent communication. This is how it can be with Jesus. We can come into such a depth of relationship that we do not always need to be talking to Him but can just enjoy His Presence, knowing He is with us and occasionally saying something like, 'Thank You, Lord Jesus' or 'I love You, Jesus'. The wonderful thing about telling somebody we love them is that they usually reply, 'I love you too.' The more we say 'I love You' to Jesus, the more we become aware of His love for us. Recently I was talking to somebody about telling Jesus we love Him as often as possible and they said, 'But I don't **feel** that way.' We don't necessarily have to feel anything because love is a commitment, a decision we make. When I got married I made a commitment before God that I would love my husband, 'for richer for poorer, for better for worse, in sickness and in health, till death us do part.' When I'm tired or have a headache I don't always feel very loving towards him. There is the odd occasion when I do not really like him, but I still love him. I'm committed to love him. If our children do something naughty we don't like what they are doing and we don't particularly **feel** any love for them at that time, but it does not mean we stop loving them. We are committed to them and love them anyway. I don't have to **feel** anything to say to Jesus that I love Him because I have made a commitment to love Him. In fact, it is easy to praise Jesus when something good has happened and we feel like it, but it is much more a *'sacrifice of praise'* (Hebrews 13:15) when we don't feel like it!

There is another way of praying that is very important which I have talked about in *What Do YOU Want, Lord?* (pages 58–61). When we get baptised in the Holy Spirit we receive a special prayer language which most people call the gift of tongues. (Read: Acts 2:4, 10:45–6, 19:6; Luke 11:9–13; 1 Corinthians 14:2–4; Jude 20/21.) This gift is so wonderful for a variety of reasons and will be extremely useful in the last days. The gift of tongues is a language or several different languages supernaturally given to us by God without us having to learn them. Although many people only use one 'unknown' tongue I believe we can reach out in faith for more than one. I have never tried to memorise the words or sounds that I'm uttering when I speak in tongues but I have definitely noticed that I use a different language in different circumstances. For example, the language I speak when I am worshipping Jesus sounds very different from when I'm doing spiritual warfare and different again when I'm praying for somebody.

I think that mostly we speak in tongues of angels but for certain situations the Lord may give us known languages of men (1 Corinthians 13:1). I've heard of people speaking a language they never learned or giving a message in tongues in a meeting, and a foreigner who has heard it has said they understood every word because they were speaking their language. In the end times we do not know what kind of difficult situations we may be in but it could be that speaking in a tongue will really help.

One time my husband was in the Belgian Congo (now Zaire) and there were a lot of rebels on the roads. Doug was driving a truck loaded with cement and suddenly came across a large tree-trunk blocking the road. When he stopped the truck a gang of rebels came out of the bush brandishing rifles and forced him out of the truck. They wanted his money but he didn't have any and was not even wearing a watch because he had been warned about these bandits. The men got very angry when they saw that Doug had no valuables they could steal from him, and they forced him into a hut at gun-point. Of course, Doug was rather afraid and thought they were going to kill him. He had been praying in tongues under his breath but then he felt the Lord tell him to speak in tongues out loud. He did so and it came out quite forcefully as though he was preaching. He did not understand a word he was saying but it soon became apparent that the rebels understood because their whole attitude changed. They dropped their rifles and started bowing to him saying 'Yes, bwana; yes, bwana,' backing out of the door and waving for him to leave! He continued speaking in 'tongues' as he made a hasty exit, climbed back into the truck and drove away, absolutely amazed at how the Lord had delivered him! Although Doug hardly knew any Swahili at the time, he realised that the Lord had supernaturally given him the language when he was in trouble. Later, when he was out of danger and he tried to speak Swahili, he couldn't speak more than a few scriptures he had already learnt and he had to preach to the people through an interpreter just as he had done before. I believe that the Lord Jesus can do this for any one of us if the need arises, whether it is in a dangerous situation now or in the last days.

The gift of tongues is so useful because it by-passes our minds and our own intellect. It is the Holy Spirit praying through us and is therefore a perfect prayer. Romans 8:26–27 says,

> 'The Spirit also helps in our weaknesses. For we do not know what we should pray for as we ought, but the Spirit Himself makes intercession for us with groanings which cannot be uttered. Now He who searches the hearts knows what the mind of the Spirit is, because He makes intercession for the saints according to the will of God.'

When there is any difficult situation or when I am going to speak at a meeting, I can pray in English for the things I think are necessary but it is only the Lord Jesus who really knows what is needed. When I am praying for somebody I do not always know the exact circumstances or problem but if I pray in tongues I know I am praying directly into the situation and that the Holy Spirit is praying through me. He can also show me how to pray in English.

There are many times when I have not known what to do or what to say, but after I have spoken in tongues for a few minutes (maybe out loud but often quietly under my breath if other people are around), I have found that a thought comes to me very clearly. Even as I am writing this, when there is something I don't know how to express on paper I will pray in tongues, sometimes for only a minute or two and sometimes much longer, until my mind is clear and the words start to flow again. Similarly, many has been the occasion when I have felt the need to pray and not known why so I've prayed in tongues and later found that the Lord has led me to be in the right place at the right time to meet somebody in need. If we need the help of the Holy Spirit to pray through us now, when things are going well, how much more will we need His help in the future when things may be much more difficult?

Tongues is also a wonderful way of keeping in close communion with Jesus, even when there is no apparent reason for praying – no apparent difficulty and no specific person that I know needs prayer. I can pray in tongues wherever and whenever I want to, silently or out loud, and know that the Holy Spirit is praying through me, either in worship to Jesus, in prayer for others, or in prayer for some unknown situation just round the corner. When I am in this kind of communion with Jesus I know He will lead me to do or say whatever He wants. I know that He will instruct me and teach me in the way I should go; He will guide me with His eye (Psalm 32:8).

Glory to Jesus!

Chapter 7

Be Not Conformed to This World

In the chapter on reading the Bible I talked about having our minds renewed and this is so necessary if we are to be transformed and not conformed to this world.

> *'I beseech you therefore, brethren, by the mercies of God, that you present your bodies a living sacrifice, holy, acceptable to God, which is your reasonable service. And do not be conformed to this world, but be transformed by the renewing of your mind, that you may prove what is that good and acceptable and perfect will of God.'*
> (Romans 12:1–2)

Some people may ask why we should not be conformed to this world. Being conformed to this world means we do what everybody else does. There is a spirit in the world which tells us what is 'normal' and acceptable – normal and acceptable to the world that is, not to God. Doing what 'everybody else' does and thinking how 'everybody else' thinks is not acceptable to God, not pleasing to Him because instead, He wants us to be *'conformed to the image of His Son'* (Romans 8:29), doing and thinking the way Jesus does. However, the spirit of the world affects us more than we realise.

When Doug and I came to Hong Kong we had no idea what the Lord wanted us to do but we wanted His will and we presented our bodies to Him to do whatever He told us to do. After we'd been here for a year or two we started to feel the pressure of other people's expectations. One Chinese young man would frequently telephone us and ask us what we were doing and how many people we had in our church. Somebody else who received our newsletters complained that we didn't say what we were doing for the Lord. Apart from not wanting to talk about the things **we** were doing but about the things **God** was doing, much of the time there was very little to report. In the eyes of the world we really did not seem to be doing very much for Jesus. This, coupled with the fact that we had run out of money, made us question whether we were in God's will or not.

'Are we in the right place, Lord? Please show us! Do You still want us in Hong Kong? If not, show us what You **do** want, Lord! And we can't go anywhere else unless You provide the money! Please speak to us, Lord!'

Every time we cried out to God like this, and it happened every few weeks, He would speak to us very clearly through that day's Bible readings. One time it was,

> *'No man, having put his hand to the plough, and looking back, is fit for the kingdom of God.'* (Luke 9:62)

'OK Lord! Please forgive us for doubting.'

The Scripture *'We walk by faith, not by sight'* (2 Corinthians 5:7), became so important to me. I knew we had to continue even if I did not see anything happening. By faith I had to believe we were in the right place doing the right things. Our responsibility was to obey the Lord. The results were **His** responsibility.

It was about that time that we went to a three-day conference at the local Youth With A Mission base and we were really blessed and refreshed with the spiritual depth of the teaching. In our next newsletter we wrote:

One of the speakers, Dean Sherman, talked about the 'spirit of the world'. 1 John 5:19 says,

> *'We know that we are the children of God, and that the whole world is under the control of the evil one.'* (NIV)

Of course the paradox to this is in Psalm 24:1,

> *'The earth is the Lord's, and the fullness thereof; the world
> and they that dwell therein.'*   (KJV)

The truth is that the world belongs to Jesus but we have let
Satan control too much of it. This spirit of the world is like
an atmosphere which pervades everything and we can be
affected by it without realising it. We need a revelation
from the Holy Spirit to be able to recognise what it is and
when it is affecting our thoughts and attitudes in ways we
have always thought alright because everybody else does
the same. When we get born-again and filled with the Holy
Spirit many of our thoughts and values change, but it
seems that there are other areas of our lives in which we
are slower to recognise this spirit of the world.

Dean Sherman talked about two main areas where we
can be affected. The first is to do with 'position'. We tend
to think that if a person has a high position or a high
qualification, then he/she is 'somebody'. They have value.
If a person is the managing director of a well-known
company or a world-famous evangelist, we will take note of
what they say more than somebody we have never heard
of before. (Some people think that because I have written a
book, I am somebody special! I am no different and no
more 'spiritual' than many other Christians!) Many of us, in
turn, want to be somebody. To get a good job we need to
have the right degrees and qualifications. We consequently
think that to do a mighty work for the Lord we also need
high qualifications from Bible College or a theological
seminary. That, however, is the way the world sees it, not
how God sees it:

> *'For that which is highly esteemed among men is an
> abomination in the sight of God.'*   (Luke 16:15)

[It is Jesus who ordains us, not man. In John 15:16 He says,
*'I have chosen you, and **ordained** you, that ye should go and
bring forth fruit'* (KJV).]

So how should we see it? The first part of the verse, 1
John 5:19, says that we are the children of God. John 1:12
says that *'as many as received* [Jesus] *to them gave He power
to become the sons of God'* (KJV). Surely there is no higher

position or qualification than that! God sets such a high value on all of us who receive Jesus as our Lord and Saviour, that He has made us His sons! Hallelujah! We are *'joint heirs with Christ'* (Romans 8:17)!

The second point that Dean Sherman talked about was 'performance'. We feel we have to live up to a certain standard before we will be accepted. We have to dress a certain way or do certain things before this group or that group will recognise us as one of them. Some men worry if they will be a good enough husband. Some women are concerned about being a good enough wife. Will I be man enough? Will I be woman enough? But whose standards are we going by? Usually by men and women we have seen portrayed in books or in films and at conferences. What sort of car have you got? What area do you live in? What do you do in the church? What denomination are you? All this is really the spirit of the world!

I used to feel useless as Doug's wife because I was not what I thought people expected me to be as a minister's wife. Minister's wives usually play the piano or organ in the services, teach children's Sunday School, arrange the flowers, have a ladies knitting circle and bake cakes. I do not play any musical instrument (Doug does); I do not have a children's ministry (Doug does); I cannot arrange flowers, knit or bake (Doug cannot either)! Now, however, I have realised that I do not have to be and do what man expects me to be and do. Some godly men in the seventeenth century produced the Westminster Confession which states: 'Man's chief end is to glorify God, and to enjoy Him forever,' so we do not have to let this spirit of the world condemn us because we are not what others expect us to be. We only have to obey God and do the things He wants us to do. Doug and I are realising that as missionaries here in Hong Kong, we do not have to live up to man's expectations or feel that we have to write home about any fantastic ministry and how many people have got saved. No! We have to do what Jesus wants and be responsible to Him, even if nobody else will ever know about it and even if we do not see the results ourselves.

That requires faith, but it also means we are free to be what God created us to be. We also know, of course, that any 'good works' that the Lord has not told us to do will go up in smoke like wood, hay and stubble when all our works are tried by fire at the Judgement Seat of Christ (1 Corinthians 3:9–15).

That message about the spirit of the world was so encouraging to me and set me free from being concerned about what other people expected of me and it is particularly important as we prepare for the end times. I believe the gap between what the world (including many Christians) expects us to do, and what Jesus calls us to do, will get wider and wider as that time draws nearer. We must allow the Cross to work in our lives. Galatians 6:14 says,

> 'God forbid that I should boast except in the cross of our Lord Jesus Christ, by whom **the world has been crucified to me**, and I to the world.'

I am reminded of a short saying:

> 'Life is short, 'twill soon be past. Only what's done for Jesus will last.'   (author unknown)

However, I do not feel even this is totally correct. We can do many things for Jesus – in fact, we can spend our whole lives working for Jesus; preaching, going to unreached tribes to evangelise, working night and day to help the under-privileged – and receive the recognition and admiration of men. But in the end, on Judgement Day, Jesus may turn around and say

> 'I never knew you: depart from Me, ye that work iniquity.'   (Matthew 7:23, KJV)

How can this be? How could Jesus say this to people who have prophesied in His Name and cast out devils or done many other wonderful works in His Name (verse 22)? The answer lies in the preceding verse;

> 'Not everyone who says to Me, "Lord, Lord" shall enter the kingdom of heaven, **but he who does the will of My Father in heaven.'**

These are strong words. Does Jesus mean that not everybody who **thinks** they will go to heaven, will make it? In the same chapter He says,

> 'Enter the **narrow** gate; for wide is the gate and broad is the way that leads to destruction, and there are many who go in by it. Because narrow is the gate and difficult is the way which leads to life, and there are few who find it.' (Matthew 7:13–14)

It is not what we do for Jesus that counts, but doing what He tells us to do, when He tells us and how.

> 'Has the Lord as great delight in burnt offerings and sacrifices, as in obeying the voice of the Lord? Behold, to obey is better than sacrifice, and to heed than the fat of rams.' (1 Samuel 15:22)

Knowing what the Lord Jesus wants us to do, knowing His will, stems from our relationship with Him. As I mentioned before, when Jesus said, 'I never knew you' He meant He never had a meaningful relationship with us which, even in natural terms, involves **two**-way communication, not just one person talking and the other listening, but both talking and listening to each other. When we are speaking about being ready, being prepared for the end times, this is perhaps the most important aspect. Do we have a meaningful relationship with Jesus? We may say that we know Jesus, but does He know us? Does He recognise us as His friends and people He can rely on to do His will? In Genesis 18:19 (KJV), God says of Abraham,

*'For **I know him**, that he will command his children and his household after him, and they shall keep the way of the Lord, to do justice and judgement; that the Lord may bring upon Abraham that which He hath spoken of him.'*

Can God say that of us? Does He know that we will do justice and judgement no matter what the personal cost?

Also, knowing what Jesus wants us to do and actually doing it are two different things. When we have spent time with Him, listening to Him to find out what He wants us to do, we then need to put it into practice – and that requires faith. Whatever Jesus tells us to do, whether through His Word, through those in authority over us, or by speaking directly into our thoughts (providing it agrees with Scripture – the Lord will **never** tell us to do something that is contrary to His written Word), we must mix it with faith. We must believe that Jesus is speaking to us. If we are not sure that we are hearing correctly, especially when it is a big thing or will affect other people, we should ask the Lord for more scripture to confirm it. It needs to be at least two or three separate verses from our normal daily Bible readings, and then we should ask advice from mature Christians like the elders in the church because, *'in the multitude of counsellors there is safety'* (Proverbs 11:14).

In that same newsletter that I just quoted from, we also wrote:

Somebody showed us a book that was written for potential missionaries, in dedication to a young lady who had been on the mission-field for a year or two. This lady had failed so miserably, in her own mind, to live up to the standards that she thought a missionary ought to, and that she thought other people expected of her, that she committed suicide! The 'spirit of the world' had deceived her into thinking that she had to have an established ministry within at least one year of going to the mission-field, when

73

in fact, like most people, she was still trying to adjust to the different culture and still struggling with language study. Obviously nobody else around her had been honest enough to talk about **their** difficulties. Perhaps they were also deceived into thinking they were not good missionaries if they had problems and they did not want anybody else to know about it in case they were considered a failure. We need to be open and honest with each other and stop pretending to be something we are not, or something we think is expected of us.

> 'If we walk in the light as He is in the light, we have fellowship with one another, and the Blood of Jesus Christ His Son cleanses us from all sin.' (1 John 1:7)

The spirit of the world has so pervaded our churches and religious organisations that we still go by man's standards instead of God's. In Mark 8:31–33, Jesus was telling the disciples that He was going to suffer and be killed. When Peter rebuked Him for this, Jesus turned round and said,

> 'Get thee behind Me, Satan: for thou savourest not the things that be of God, but the things that be of men.' (KJV)

J.B. Phillips' translation puts it:

> '. . . you are not looking at things from God's point of view.'

Sometimes we think we are, until the Lord shows us that we have been seeing things from a church's point of view or a denomination's point of view. We are so much surrounded by this spirit of the world that we do not see how it has even crept into our ministries. We need a revelation from the Holy Spirit to show us where our ways and our thoughts differ from His. We need to study the Bible to find out God's thoughts – even on such basic matters as finance. We all know the verse,

> 'God shall supply all your need according to His riches in glory by Christ Jesus.' (Philippians 4:19)

The spirit of the world has caught us up so subtly that we don't realise that when we tell others about our needs, we are not trusting God. We **think** we are. Yes, God uses people to meet the needs but if we are truly trusting Him, we only tell **Him** – and **He** tells the people. What we are really doing is saying, 'Yes, God can – but I can't trust Him to tell others I have a need so I'll do it for Him'! We see that so many other people do it that way, including many well-known Christians with very big ministries, that it must be alright. Some may say, 'But what if the people can't hear from the Lord, or aren't listening?' The Bible says,

> 'Whatever is not from faith is sin.'   (Romans 14:23)

Philippians 4:6 says,

> 'Be anxious for nothing, but in everything by prayer and supplication, with thanksgiving, let your requests be made known to **God**.'

Not man! Then verse 7 shows us the result of doing it God's way:

> 'And the peace of God, which surpasses all understanding, will guard your hearts and minds through Christ Jesus.'

If there comes a time that there is a postal strike, or such an economic depression that nobody else has any money either, then it will be useless looking to man for help. This will apply even more when those days come *'that no one may buy or sell except one who has the mark or the name of the beast, or the number of his name ... 666'* (Revelation 13:17–18). Only Jesus will be able to help us and it would be wise to start practising this now, depending only on Him. George Muller trusted God to provide for two thousand orphans. Hudson Taylor, founder of the China Inland Mission which is now known as the Overseas Missionary Fellowship, trusted God to provide workers to go into every province of China, mainly where missionaries had never been before, and to provide the funds to support them. Neither of these nineteenth century men of God ever made appeals for money or made their financial needs known. It is true that after their ministries grew, there were many people who knew about their work and we can think, 'It's OK for them, but nobody knows about me.' But these men proved the truth of the saying, '**Where God guides, He provides**' well before anybody knew about them. They hung on to the promise of Matthew. 6:32–33,

> *'For your heavenly Father knows that you need all these things. But seek first the kingdom of God and His righteousness, and all these things shall be added to you.'*

They were not dependent on the people of God but the God of the people who knew their needs even before they themselves did. The Lord Jesus was very real to them and they knew His love and faithfulness. If Jesus Christ **is** *'the same yesterday, and today, and forever'* (Hebrews 13:8), then why can't we trust Him to provide all our needs like He has promised, and like those men and women of old did? We can only do so if we continually mix those promises with faith.

Another area in our lives in which we must be careful not to be conformed to this world is in boy–girl relationships. The spirit of the world has so affected everybody with its permissiveness that most young people of today, even after they have become Christians, do not know what behaviour is acceptable or not acceptable to God.

Chapter 8

Holiness

When we are considering how we should prepare ourselves for the end times, holiness is essential. Hebrews 12:14 says,

> *'Pursue peace with all people, and **holiness**, **without which no one will see the Lord.**'*

Isaiah, when talking about God's Kingdom, says,

> *'A highway shall be there, and a road,*
> *And it shall be called the **Highway of Holiness**.*
> *The unclean shall not pass over it . . .*
> *But the redeemed shall walk there.'*   (Isaiah 35:8–9)

Holiness does not mean being perfect. In Young's concordance it says it means 'being **separate**, **set apart** for God'. It means we **want** Jesus to be in complete control of our lives. When we are fully committed to Jesus, He is fully committed to us! Holiness means we want the will of God in every area of our lives and **want** Him to show us if there is any area in our lives that we are still hanging on to which hinders our relationship with Him.

It also means we **want** to be right with Jesus. We want to please Him and we do not want to do anything that would hurt Him or His Name. We want Him to be glorified and we want our lives to glorify Him so that other people can see how wonderful Jesus is.

There is a saying that goes, 'Cleanliness is next to godliness.' Being clean in every area of our lives is part of being godly. Psalm 4:3 says,

> *'Know that the Lord has set apart for Himself him who is godly.'*

To be holy, set apart by God for Himself, means we are clean in thought, word and deed. It is not a sin to have a wrong thought, but it **is** a sin if we **entertain** that thought and keep dwelling on it. We must cast down *'arguments* [imaginations] *and every high thing that exalts itself against the knowledge of God,* **bringing every thought into captivity** *to the obedience of Christ'* (2 Corinthians 10:5). We do not have to be controlled by our thoughts. In the Name of Jesus we can rebuke satan for giving us the wrong thoughts and ask Jesus to cleanse us by His Blood and fill us afresh with His **Holy** Spirit.

One area where holiness is particularly important is sex. For those of us who are already married, the Bible very clearly shows us that adultery is sin – even to look on a woman with lust in our hearts (Matthew 5:28) is seen by God as adultery. For people who are not married, especially those who are expecting that they will one day find their life partner, it is so important that we find the right one – the one God has prepared for us – and that we know how to behave before we are married so we do not mar our relationship with our partner and with Jesus. The end times are going to be difficult enough anyway, without being 'stuck' with the wrong one or starting off 'on the wrong foot'.

Everybody wants to be happily married to someone who will fulfil all their dreams but this will never happen unless we first find our fulfilment in Jesus! No matter how wonderful, how 'perfect' we think somebody is, they will never be able to meet all our needs. Only Jesus can meet all our needs. Only Jesus understands our deepest longings. If we look to any human being to fulfil us we will only be disappointed and disillusioned; after all – they are only human!

There is nothing wrong, however, in wanting to be married. In fact, it would be unusual **not** to want to get married. The important thing is to get married to the right person at the right time. So many of the people who come to us for counselling are contemplating marriage or feel trapped in a marriage that is going wrong.

So how do we find the right person? I would like to list some of the major points to consider before any person, young or not so young, single or divorced, gets married:

1. The first thing we need to know is what Jesus tells us about this in the Bible.

> *'Do not be yoked together with unbelievers. For what do righteousness and wickedness have in common? Or what fellowship can light have with darkness? ... What does a believer have in common with an unbeliever?'* (2 Corinthians 6:14–15, NIV)

Also read Ezra 9:1–2 and 11–12. In plain English that means a Christian should not marry a non-Christian.

2. Why? This is shown very clearly in two scriptures:

> *'Make no treaty* [covenant] *with them...'*
> (Exodus 23:32)

> *'Do not intermarry with them. Do not give your daughters to their sons or take their daughters for your sons, for they will turn your sons away from following Me to serve other gods, and the Lord's anger will burn against you...'* (Deuteronomy 7:3–4, NIV)

Someone may now say, 'But my boyfriend/girlfriend doesn't worship idols.' Anything we put before Jesus is an idol, a false god, because Jesus must be Number One in our lives. In Colossians 1:18 Paul said, *'... that in all things He* [Jesus] *might have the pre-eminence.'* Anything that comes before Jesus, including our work, computer, car, sport, house, television, partner, children, money, or even our ministry, is an idol. There is nothing wrong with these things in themselves but if we put them before Jesus it is an abomination in the sight of God: (Exodus 20:3, Deuteronomy 7:25).

As I already mentioned we become like the people we spend time with.

'He who walks with wise men will be wise, but the companion of fools will be destroyed.'

(Proverbs 13:20)

Therefore, as Christians we should spend time with people we want to become like, people whose lives are a challenge to us to draw closer to Jesus. That does not mean that we should not have anything to do with non-Christians, but we should not spend more time with them than necessary. Our closest friends need to be Christians. If our spouse is to be our closest friend, after Jesus, then we need to be able to share with him/her the issues that matter most to us, such as spiritual things. We need to have the same values, especially so that we can help and encourage each other during the difficult times ahead. We need to be able to support each other spiritually so there is harmony in the home even if there is persecution outside the home. [Don't worry if you became a Christian after you got married and your spouse is not yet a believer. Read 1 Corinthians 7:12–17 and my chapter on Household Salvation.]

3. So whom should we marry? Amos 3:3 says,

'Can two walk together, except they be agreed?'

Not only should our life-partner be a Christian, but if we are 'sold out' to the Lord Jesus then we should seek to marry somebody who is also 'sold out' to the Lord. We need to find somebody with whom we agree spiritually, particularly on major doctrines such as healing, baptism in the Holy Spirit, baptism in the Name of the Lord Jesus Christ, deliverance etc., as recorded in the Bible, especially the Acts of the Apostles, and who also has the same views on the end-times.

Cross-cultural marriages can also be very difficult. I am certainly not saying that we should not marry somebody of a different nationality or culture, but we must first consider the problems we may face. People of different cultures often **think** differently, and can have different values. Their sense of humour may be different and it is essential to be able to laugh together! Another consideration is language. If one or both partners are not speaking in their first language there may be even more misunderstandings and lack of communication than usual. So think carefully before getting involved with somebody of a different culture. This is not racial prejudice. In Jesus

> '...there is neither Greek nor Jew, circumcised nor uncircumcised, barbarian, Scythian, slave nor free, but Christ is all and in all.'   (Colossians 3:11)

After we were married, Doug and I became very aware that we were from different backgrounds. We are both British and were raised in England, but I was brought up in a traditional Jewish home and he wasn't; I had been living in Israel for a few years and he hadn't. It took us some time to adjust! Without God's help we may not have made it! It is only thanks to Jesus and His grace that we did, but we still have to keep working at it!

4. It is a good idea to ask God for what we want our partner to be like **before** we become involved with anyone. When we are emotionally involved with someone it is almost impossible to hear God's voice when we ask Him if this person is to be our life-partner, because we have already decided what we want the answer to be. Before we can hear the Lord's voice on any issue we must be truly willing to hear whatever He says. Satan is very good at whispering, 'Well, they say they are a Christian and they do go to

church.' When we are emotionally involved we will easily believe this because it is what we **want** to hear and believe. But they might be doing this just to please us and will not make any pretence at being a Christian after we are married.

One young lady went to her pastor and said, 'This is the young man I'm going to marry.'

'Is he a Christian?' the pastor asked.

'No; but he will be after we are married. He promised.'

The pastor asked the young lady to stand on the table. Then he told her to take the man's hand and pull him up onto the table. Then he said to the man, 'You pull her down.'

Who do you think won?

The pastor said, 'That's what happens to most people.'

5. What kind of person should we ask the Lord for? I feel we should be specific. How do we know we have found the right person if we do not know what we are looking for?

> *'Ask, and it will be given to you.'*   (Luke 11:9)

> *'Ask, and you will receive, that your joy may be full.'*
> (John 16:24)

We should ask for the things that we think are important to us, the things that we really feel are essential, or we will easily change our minds if we are attracted to somebody who does not meet the requirements. For me, the most important thing was that he was a man of God who was in love with Jesus. It is good for a woman to marry a man who is spiritually as mature or more mature than herself, who she can respect spiritually, because he should be the head of the family. Both of you should have a similar or compatible vision or calling. For example, it may be best for a man who is called to be a pastor to ask for a woman who would be happy to be a pastor's wife and who can help him in the ministry. If he is already a pastor it may not be good for him to marry a new Christian unless she is really hungry for more of Jesus and grows quickly or he may find himself having to 'baby-sit' all the time. A man who is called to be an evangelist should perhaps ask for a woman who does not mind her husband being away for long periods of time while she stays at home to look after the children. Otherwise he needs to be prepared to have his wife and children travel with him – that is unless they both agree not to have children. A man or woman who feels the Lord is calling them to be a missionary to a certain country must find a partner who either has the same calling or is willing to be 100% behind them – remembering that a woman's primary calling is to be a helpmeet to her husband.

Prayerfully, before the Lord, we should ask Him what else **He** wants for us, not what we think would be good. If we delight ourselves in the **Lord**, He will give us the desires of our hearts (Psalm 37:4). If our delight is not in Jesus, we may not get the marriage partner that we want.

'You ask and do not receive, because you ask amiss.'
(James 4:3)

To one person He might impress that their partner be musical; to another, that they be in 'full-time' ministry. I am Jewish so it was important for me that my husband loves the Jewish people and understands God's plan for them and for Israel. I am not talking about minor things, such as what colour their hair is or how tall they are – though a very tall lady would probably be more comfortable with a man who is also very tall. This is a serious issue because we are going to spend the rest of our lives with this person!

6. After we have asked the Lord for these things we should then commit our future partner to Him to prepare. Any time it comes to our mind we should not be anxious at how long it seems we are waiting. God's timing is perfect. Philippians 4:6–7 applies again:

> *'Be anxious for nothing, but in everything by prayer and supplication, with thanksgiving, let your requests be made known to God; and the peace of God, which surpasses all understanding, will guard your hearts and minds through Christ Jesus.'*

[This is a good scripture to memorise.]

Believe me, the right partner is worth waiting for no matter how old you are. I was thirty-three when I got married, and I know many others who have even been in their forties or fifties. That does not mean if you are twenty now, that you will necessarily have to wait another ten or twenty years. God's plan is different for everybody and His plan is always the best. We can trust Him to bring the right one along at the right time. The wrong one is the worst mistake you can ever make. Marriage should be for a lifetime. Divorce is not an easy way out and God hates divorce! (Malachi 2:16).

7. What should we do if we meet somebody we like? We should first ask ourselves if they fit what we asked God for. If not, we must totally forget them. Remember – the things we asked for were important to us at the time so they should still be important to us now. If we asked for somebody who loves Jesus with all their heart when we were twenty years old, that should still be our priority even though a few years have passed and we are not so young anymore and

are afraid we will never find the right one. We must not settle for second best – we will regret it for the rest of our lives!

If the person does meet the requirements, then **before** we go out with them, we should still ask the Lord if this is the one **He** has for us. If we truly want God's will in our lives, before we ask Him we must examine ourselves to see if we are really willing to hear his answer, 'Yes' or 'No'. If the answer is 'No', there is no need to worry. It means that the Lord has someone even better for us!

8. How do we hear what God is saying to us on this important issue? Who we marry is probably the most important decision we will ever make and affects our whole future so we cannot be too careful about hearing the Lord correctly. Being attracted to somebody, and a friend saying, 'Oh, you really suit each other!' is not a strong enough basis on which to marry. For such a major decision, to go by what we feel or by what other people say is not enough.

> *'In the mouth of two or three witnesses shall every word be established.'*　　　　　　(2 Corinthians 13:1)

We need a minimum of three scriptures to confirm it. These should be from our normal daily Bible readings or perhaps through somebody who knows nothing about the situation. We should not go searching through the Bible to find a verse that says what we want it to say! The day that I asked the Lord Jesus if Doug was the one He wanted me to marry, it was the 11th January. In that day's readings I read,

> *'... this is he ...'*　　　　　　　　　　(Matthew 11:10)

> *'He who has ears to hear, let him hear.'*
> 　　　　　　　　　　　　　　　　(Matthew 11:15)

When I argued with the Lord, He replied through verse 17,

> *'We played the flute for you, and you did not dance; we mourned to you, and you did not lament.'*

(That is, 'You asked for a husband, and now that I'm giving you one, you argue with Me! You're never satisfied!') Then I said to the Lord, 'I know he loves the Jewish people, but does it matter that he is not Jewish himself?' The reply came in the next chapter I read, Acts 11:9,

> *'What God has cleansed you must not call common [unclean].'*

This verse also answered my query as to whether it mattered that Doug was divorced. (I have written in more detail about how the Lord showed me I was to marry Doug in my first book, *What Do YOU Want, Lord?*) It is interesting to note that when I had first asked Jesus if my future husband needed to be Jewish or not, I never got a reply. At the time we got married Doug did not know that he was half Jewish. It has come to light more recently that his father was Jewish but was brought up by a non-Jewish, atheist step-father who did not allow his mother to follow the Jewish traditions. If the Lord had told me that my husband should be Jewish I would have thought that Doug was the wrong one. On the other hand, if He had told me that my husband would not be Jewish, later, after we were married and we had found out that he is, I would have thought I had made a mistake! So when the Lord Jesus does not answer our questions, there is always a good reason for it even if we cannot see it at the time!

9. On the same day that I was asking the Lord about Doug, also in the Bible readings was Proverbs 11:14,

> *'. . . in the multitude of counsellors there is **safety**.'*

This is very important. We should go to the elders of the church with the scriptures the Lord has given us, and ask them to pray and see if the Lord shows them that it is right. If they disagree we should ask God again. If it is truly God's will, then He will give us two or three more scriptures and will also change the elders' minds providing we have the right attitude.

10. Why do we need scriptures? To counteract the devil's doubts, before and after marriage. If we have any big arguments or difficulties we have something firm to stand on. We can say to the devil, 'Look! It is written!' We can be sure that the Lord has put us together and therefore He can and will help us to get through the difficulties. Having the elders' support is also necessary because we know they will be praying for us and they can help us find a way through any problems.

11. How should we behave before marriage? The Bible is very clear that we should not be sexually involved before marriage.

> *'Flee sexual immorality ... your body is the temple of the Holy Spirit ... therefore glorify God in your body.'*
> (1 Corinthians 6:18–20).

> *' ... avoid sexual immorality ... for God did not call us to be impure but to live a holy life.'*
> (1 Thessalonians 4:1–8, NIV)

I believe this does not just mean that a man and a woman should not have sexual intercourse before marriage, but also that they should not touch each other in a way that would arouse them sexually. Paul said,

> *'It is good for a man not to touch a woman.'*
> (1 Corinthians 7:1)

Girls must remember that men are aroused much more quickly than themselves and should therefore not tempt the man in any way, even in the way they dress. Both should make sure they are not in tempting situations and *'make no provision for the flesh, to fulfil its lusts'* (Romans 13:14). To be alone in a house can be asking for trouble, and we can talk privately just as easily over a cup of coffee in McDonalds or walking in a busy street. And not only should we be careful to act in a holy way, but we must also make sure our thoughts are clean and holy. Wrong actions usually start in our thoughts!

12. If in doubt about how to behave, we should ask ourselves, 'What would Jesus do?'

13.   *'What God has joined together, let man not separate.'*
    (Mark 10:9)

If we want God to join us together in 'holy' matrimony, we must be sure we are living holy lives! A church wedding with all the right words, does not guarantee that God is there. How can the Holy God join together two people who are living sinfully?

14. A final test to think about before getting married is this: our partner should take us closer to Jesus, not take up all our time and thoughts and draw us away from Him! If we find we are thinking more about a person than we are of Jesus, then perhaps we should finish the relationship. As I mentioned before, Jesus must be number one in our lives.

PART THREE

Hindrances

Chapter 9

Sin

If we are talking about how to maintain an intimate love relationship with Jesus, we must also talk about a few of the hindrances. I have touched on some of these points before but now I want to talk about them in more detail. Sin may seem obvious but I think it is still worth mentioning.

> *'Who may ascend into the hill of the Lord?*
> *Or who may stand in His holy place?*
> *He who has clean hands and a pure heart,*
> *Who has not lifted up his soul to an idol,*
> *Nor sworn deceitfully.*
> *He shall receive blessing from the Lord,*
> *And righteousness from the God of his salvation.'*
>
> (Psalm 24:3–5)

Perhaps sin is the biggest of all hindrances and we must hate it – not somebody else's sin but our own. We must be willing to deal with anything in our lives that is not pleasing to the Lord, as soon as He shows it to us, even if it is something that everybody does. Just because everybody else does it, does not make it any less sin. We tend to think of big sins and little sins, but in God's eyes, sin is sin. The so called big sins, like murder, adultery, and stealing, we all know are wrong and of course, good Christians like you and I would never do those things. But the Bible says,

> *'Whoever hates his brother is a murderer.'*
>
> (1 John 3:15)

Which one of us has never hated somebody? The Bible is also very strong when it says,

'Whoever looks at a woman [or man] *to lust for her has already committed adultery with her in his heart.'*

(Matthew 5:28)

That means there are far more people who have committed adultery than think they have! Stealing, too, covers far more than robbing a bank or taking money out of somebody's purse. Taking pens home from the office is stealing! Not saying anything when we have been given too much change at the supermarket is stealing!

But what about the 'little' sins in my life? It is so easy to cover up the little sins because nobody else knows about them. But Jesus knows about them and it is the little sins, *'the little foxes, that spoil the vines'* (Song of Solomon 2:15). It is the so-called little sins that spoil our relationship with Jesus.

'If I regard iniquity in my heart,
The Lord will not hear.'

(Psalm 66:18)

I know that there is a definite barrier between myself and Jesus when I criticise somebody, when I am selfish or when I worry. It is not until I confess my sin to the Lord and ask Him to forgive me and cleanse me by His Blood, that I can feel His Presence again. In fact, He has been wanting to deal with my selfishness for a long time but it is only recently that I have really allowed Him to. For years He was telling me that I am selfish and I knew He was right (of course!). My response was always, 'Yes, I'm sorry, Lord. Please forgive me and please change me.' But it is only recently, that I have been determined, that I have really meant business when I have said I do not want to be selfish. Now I have asked the Lord Jesus to show me each time I am selfish. Then I can do something about it immediately! I can ask the Lord to forgive me and to help me, so that, by His grace, I can stop doing whatever it is. Then immediately, I can be back in fellowship with Jesus again.

Recently we were invited to go somewhere for afternoon tea, and everybody was asked to take some food towards the tea. I selected two packets of biscuits we had in the cupboard and thought, 'That will do. I don't need them.' Later, after we had left home, Jesus showed me so clearly that I was being selfish again. I had other things in the house I could have taken but I did not want to have to replace them. It would be inconvenient! It was not because we did not have anything else or did not have the money to replace it, it was pure selfishness on my part. Love gives! I was horrified when Jesus showed me what garbage was in my heart and I could hardly wait to put it right. I had to tell Doug that I needed to go to the supermarket before we went to the tea. I knew I would have no peace and would not be able to have close communion with Jesus unless I went and bought something else to take. Jesus is so precious to me and having fellowship with Him is so important to me I do not want anything, no matter how small, to separate me from Him. How I thank Jesus for His mercy and His patience towards me!

Whatever the sin, it need not hinder our relationship for long because when we realise we have sinned we can do something about it immediately.

'If we confess our sins, He is faithful and just to forgive us our sins and to cleanse us from all unrighteousness.'
(1 John 1:9)

This is another good verse to memorise. We do not need to wait, in fact we must not wait, but immediately confess our wrong action, thought or attitude as sin, and ask Jesus to forgive us, to cleanse us by His Blood, and to fill us afresh with His Holy Spirit. If we do not do this immediately we are aware of our sin, the devil will come in with more rubbish – as the saying goes: 'give him an inch and he'll take a mile.' If we leave the door open even a crack, the devil will try to push it wide open, so we must close the door before he gets a chance. If we find ourselves worrying about something we should say, 'No, I'm not going to worry about this. I'm going to trust You Lord Jesus to sort the situation out.' And then give the problem to the Lord and leave it with Him. We then need to continue giving it to the Lord every time we start to worry about it again until we have truly left it with Him.

If we find anger or irritation rising in our hearts, we must immediately say to ourselves, 'No! I'm not going to get angry. I forgive them. Bless them in the Name of Jesus. And forgive me, Lord Jesus and fill me with Your love for them. Thank You, Jesus!' And then start worshipping Jesus again **as though nothing had happened**. For myself, I have found this is the most important part. It is too easy to listen to the devil's lies when he says, 'See! You've blown it again! You're no good. You'll never make it. How can you think you can have a good relationship with Jesus when you keep doing those same things?' etc. etc. But the devil is a liar and the father of lies (John 8:44) and when he exaggerates a truth he makes it a lie. I have found the best way for me to deal with those accusations is to agree with what is true but throw out the rest: 'Yes, it's true I've blown it again but, Hallelujah, when I confess my sin Jesus is faithful and just to forgive me and to cleanse me from all unrighteousness. And now I'm washed in His Blood and can enter His Presence justified – just as if I'd never sinned. Hallelujah! Glory to Jesus!' That only takes a few seconds so when we refuse to listen to the devil's lies and condemnation, the gap in our communion with Jesus need only be momentary. We must not dwell on our mistakes. Remember:

'*The truth shall make you free.*' (John 8:32)

So if something our mind tells us does not make us free but binds us up, it cannot be the truth or it is an exaggeration of the truth. Ignore it!

Chapter 10

Unforgiveness

We talked a little about forgiveness in the chapter on dealing with pain but I want to add to that because it is so important. When somebody really hurts us, whether they ask for forgiveness or not, we must forgive them. Even if they do a terrible thing or make false accusations against us, if we do not forgive them it will spoil our relationship with Jesus. It will eat away at us and cause us to become bitter. Whatever they have done, we must still forgive them. You may say, 'But how can I forgive them when what they did was so bad?' or even, 'I don't want to forgive them. They need to suffer for what they did to me (or my mother, or my brother, or my child).' But when we do not forgive somebody it is we who suffer the most:

> 'If you do not forgive men their trespasses, neither will your Father forgive your trespasses.'   (Matthew 6:15)

Many times it is impossible for us to forgive somebody in our own strength – but Jesus can do it for us. As we know, when He was hanging on the Cross as a common criminal even though He had done nothing wrong, He said of those who caused His crucifixion,

> 'Father, forgive them, for they do not know what they do.'   (Luke 23:34)

Forgiveness is not a feeling, it is a decision, an act of our will. If we find we cannot forgive somebody we can say, 'Lord, I **want** to forgive them; please help me. As an act of my will I **choose** to forgive them, in Jesus' Name.' And then, every time we think about the person or the situation and start to feel upset again, we can say, 'I forgive them in the Name of Jesus. Bless them in the Name of

Jesus. I love them in the Name of Jesus.' Sometimes I have had to do that up to a hundred times a day but when I am determined to forgive and not to harbour any resentment, the bad feelings gradually disappear. After a few days or weeks I find I can think of the person without any feelings of hurt, rejection or resentment. God's grace **is** sufficient for us (2 Corinthians 12:9) but we must make sure we react to His grace and not to the situation;

> *'Looking carefully lest anyone fall short of the grace of God; lest any root of bitterness springing up cause trouble, and by this many become defiled.'*
>
> (Hebrews 12:15)

A few years ago the Lord Jesus showed me something else about forgiveness. I was surprised when I was suddenly assailed with feelings of resentment towards somebody whose actions had hurt me many years before, whom I had long since forgiven, and with whom I had a very good on-going relationship. In my presence that person started telling somebody else about the particular incident which they knew had been so painful for me, and saying how difficult it had been for them. I was amazed that the person could talk about it in front of me with absolutely no regard for the pain it had caused me! Strong feelings of resentment welled up inside me and silently I quickly said, 'I forgive them in the Name of Jesus.' No matter how many times I said it, the resentment did not go – in fact, it seemed to get even worse. I could not understand it. I thought I had forgiven that person long before. I **knew** I had forgiven them and had praised the Lord for all He had done in my life through that situation. Then why was I feeling this way again?

I struggled with this for two or three months, continually forgiving, but continually feeling the resentment. One night I was particularly having a battle with it and was crying out to Jesus to show me why I was not getting the victory.

Suddenly, it hit me! It was so obvious! Yes, I had truly forgiven that person for all that had happened in the past. What I had not forgiven them for however, and which I needed to do, was for hurting me **again** by being so insensitive and talking about it in front of me, ignoring the fact that it had been so painful to me, although they had certainly known it. My resentment was over the recent incident, not the original one! What a relief that was as Jesus showed it to me and I whole-heartedly forgave the person concerned. The resentment disappeared instantly and I was free to love the person again. Thank You, Jesus! Not only must we forgive people for hurting us, but also we must forgive them for any insensitivity they may have concerning that.

Is there any resentment or unforgiveness in your life? No matter how badly somebody has treated you, make that decision to forgive them. Remember – forgiveness is not a feeling, it is an act of our will. If you think you **cannot** forgive somebody, but you **want** to, tell Jesus just that and ask Him to help you. He can and He will. He knows better than any of us what it is to forgive those who mistreat us.

Chapter 11

Wrong Reactions

In every situation we have a few seconds to decide how we are going to react: to God's grace or to the situation. If we react to His grace we react in our spirit with love and forgiveness. If we do not react to God's grace we react in our soul which is our mind or reasoning, our will and our emotions. To illustrate this I would like to give you just one example out of many, of when I reacted in my soul and how it affected my spiritual life for a few weeks. In this particular instance, if the Lord Jesus had not shown me the cause and helped me put it right, it would have wrecked my marriage too.

One day I woke up feeling really exhausted with barely enough energy to make a cup of tea. As there was nothing urgent to be done that day I decided I would go back to bed and rest. I started to read my Bible but my eyes would not stay open so I tried to sleep. Although I was so tired, I could not seem to drop off and my mind started going round. To stop my mind working I tried to read again but soon gave up and just lay there with my eyes closed. Suddenly it seemed as though every negative thought possible was crowding into my mind: 'I can't do anything right'; 'I always make a mess of things'; 'Why bother?'; 'What's the point?'; 'Everything's so difficult'; 'Nobody really cares'; 'I may as well give up'; and eventually 'I'd be better off dead'!

As quickly as the thoughts came I tried to reject them. In the Name of Jesus I rebuked the spirits of rejection, self-pity, condemnation and suicide etc., but I could not seem to stop the thoughts coming. I tried to speak in tongues but it did not flow. I tried to worship Jesus but I was soon battling against the negative thoughts again.

I knew it was an attack of the devil. It was years since I had thought these things and I could not understand why this was happening? Was there some unconfessed sin in my life that had opened the door for satan to come in with his hordes of demons? The Name of Jesus is far more powerful than satan and I knew the scripture *'resist the devil and he will flee from you'* was preceded by *'submit to God'* (James 4:7). Was I not submitting to God in something? Why could I not win the battle? And why did I feel so physically weak?

I asked Doug to come and pray for me. I tried to explain how weak I was feeling and what a battle I was having in my mind. He did pray for me but I didn't really feel any better. We took communion together but I was still so weak I could hardly walk and I seemed almost totally devoid of bodily strength. I had to be helped with everything and I could hardly open my eyes or talk above a whisper! I did not know what had happened to me and was beginning to get exceedingly worried, although I tried to pray and quote Scripture. Most of the time I just lay on my bed listening to tapes; I had to keep my mind off my condition. Where was Jesus? I cried out to Him to help me but it seemed He was not listening.

At the end of the second day I could stand it no longer. I knew it was the devil binding me though I did not understand how he had got an inroad into my life. I felt I should be able to 'snap out of it' and pull myself together, but I did not seem to have the physical, mental or spiritual strength to help myself. In desperation I asked Doug to hit me. He hesitated at first but when I continued to urge him, he agreed and hit me on the back, saying, 'Who are you, devil, that's binding my wife? Come on – name yourself!'

Doug continued praying for me and challenging the devil. After several minutes the spirits of insanity and fear of insanity named themselves and were cast out in the wonderful Name of Jesus. My strength came back and at last I was able to praise the Lord more freely though I still felt very tired.

During the next couple of weeks I was a lot better, except that when I tried to mentally focus on anything for more than a few minutes my mind went a complete blank. I could not think; I could not make even the simplest decision! It was so frustrating! The work was building up on my desk but I couldn't do anything about it – and worrying certainly didn't help! My mind would then start on the endless circle of negative thoughts, as I tried to overcome them with praise, and resist them in the Name of Jesus. I therefore tried to busy myself with practical things like cooking and cleaning, and anything that didn't require much thinking.

Then one day I went to a prayer meeting. I did not always go to this meeting but usually asked Jesus first if He wanted me to go. If I felt He did want me to go, I would check with Doug and make sure it was alright with him in case he wanted me to help him with something else. Sometimes we would both go. This particular time I was not sure if I should go or not, but as I woke up in plenty of time and was still feeling the need to keep occupied, I decided I would go. I did my Bible readings before I went and took another book with me to read on the bus and train to keep my mind busy. Just before I arrived at my destination I read the words: 'I must learn to *abide in my calling.*' The words were in italics and shot out of the page at me! I knew that Jesus was saying to **me**: 'Abide in your calling!'

My only response could be 'What **is** my calling, Lord?'

Immediately the thought came to me, 'To be a help-meet for Doug.'

'Oh!' I gulped. It was not what I had expected to hear but I knew it was the Lord Jesus speaking to me. Genesis 2:18 says,

> *'It is not good that the man should be alone; I will make him a help meet for him.'*

This was the scripture the Lord had first given me to show me that He wanted me to get married sometime, and in fact, that was the reason He had made me! Actually, ladies, it is the **primary** calling of all married women, whether we like it or not, even though we may also have another calling on our lives. Gentlemen – it should be emphasised that we ladies are to be a **help** to our husbands, not a servant or slave to fulfil their every demand. Yes, we are to submit to our husbands and to respect them (Ephesians 5:22–33), but the same passage of Scripture also says,

> '*Submitting* **to one another**...' (Ephesians 5:21)

and

> '*Husbands, love your wives, just as Christ also loved the church and gave Himself for it.*' (Ephesians 5:25)

It is not difficult for a wife to submit to her husband when he tells her and shows her how much he loves her!

I thought about Doug, that wonderful man of God, the best husband in the world, who loved me so much that it was not difficult to love him in return and help him. But as I thought about him I had to acknowledge that it had not been so easy the past few weeks. Something had crept in that had clouded our relationship. Oh dear!

I knew I was going to have to spend some time on my knees alone with Jesus but now I was on my way to a prayer meeting. Although I tried to push these thoughts to the back of my mind until later, I started wondering if going to this prayer meeting qualified as helping Doug. I had not consulted him about going this time; I had not even consulted Jesus about it! 'Oh dear! Then what should I do, Lord? Do You want me to go or should I just turn around and go back home?'

The first thought in my mind was 'go home'. I quickly put the Blood of Jesus on my mind and thoughts by faith and asked Jesus again. Still the answer seemed to be 'go home'.

'Well I better go home then, I suppose.'

As soon as I got home I locked myself in the bedroom and fell on my face before Jesus.

'Lord Jesus, why are You telling me to abide in my calling? In what way am I **not** being a helpmeet for Doug? What are You saying to me? Speak to me, **please.**'

Jesus spoke softly into my heart, 'You are in rebellion and *"rebellion is as the sin of witchcraft"* ' (1 Samuel 15:23).

I gulped! Those were strong words! But as I thought about it I knew it was true – I **was** in rebellion. The past few weeks I had resented helping Doug when he was outside repairing a car or doing jobs around the house, and I had deliberately avoided asking him if he needed help. But where had the rebellion come in? Then the Lord reminded me of something that had happened a couple of months previously. We had been offered a computer for only HK$200 (approx. US$25), which of course, was a real bargain, and Doug had been very eager to get it. But neither of us knew anything about computers and I knew I would be the one who was going to have to spend hours learning. Doug would leave it all to me and I felt I had enough to do without this as well. Doug insisted and I resented it! True – it would be quicker doing our newsletters and could be very useful for storing information. That is, after I got the hang of it and also learnt to type! In the meantime it would probably take twice as long, if not three times as long, to do even a straightforward letter. And anyway, who was going to teach me?

I argued; Doug insisted.

In the end I 'submitted' – but inside I was really angry. When I looked back, I could see that my attitude towards him had changed at that point. I had hardened my heart!

As the Lord Jesus showed me these things I felt so ashamed.

'Oh, Lord Jesus, I'm sorry. **I'm sorry**! Forgive me, please. Have mercy on me!'

Again He spoke to my heart, 'You are selfish. You only want to do what suits you. I have put you with Doug to do what is suitable for him; to help him whenever he needs you.'

Jesus reminded me that love is not a feeling but a decision, a commitment, and love **gives** – no matter how inconvenient it may be for myself. And Doug was so patient with me. I realised again that I have the best husband in the world – exactly right for me!

For some time I wept before the Lord, asking Him to forgive me, to set me free from the rebellion, witchcraft, selfishness and self-pity; to cleanse me by His Blood and to fill me afresh with His Holy Spirit. Peace came and I knew I was forgiven and free. Hallelujah! Thank You, Jesus!

Now, with the rebellion gone, I asked Jesus how I could be a better helpmeet for Doug. The answer came quickly:

> *'Come to Me, all you who labour and are heavy laden, and I will give you rest. Take My yoke upon you and learn from Me, for I am gentle and lowly in heart, and you will find rest for your souls. For My yoke is easy and My burden is light.'*　　　　　　　　　　　　(Matthew 11:28–30)

Yes. That was the answer alright; keeping close to Jesus, continually fellowshipping with Him and asking Him how I can be a helpmeet, suitable for Doug in each situation. Being yoked to Jesus **would** be easy if I walked close to Him, turning in obedience this way and that way as He turned. It was when I pulled to one side, rushed ahead or resisted, that it became painful – especially when I resisted! 'Help me, Lord Jesus, to keep close to You, trusting and obeying You, every minute of the day.'

During the next hour or so I stayed on my knees communing with my Jesus. He continued to throw light on why I had been having such a difficult time the past few weeks. James 4:7 says,

> *'Therefore submit to God. Resist the devil, and he will flee from you.'*

I had been trying to resist the devil but he had not been fleeing from me because of my rebellion. My rebellion against my husband, God's delegated authority, meant I was rebelling against God Himself, so the devil had had a legal right to attack me!

The devil has many ways to attack us and try to prevent us from living in the victory that Jesus has won for us on the Cross. But *'we are not ignorant of his devices'* (2 Corinthians 2:11), so we must make sure we have on *'the whole armour of God'* (Ephesians 6:10–18). If we do not seem to have the power to withstand the enemy, we must ask the Lord to show us where we have a chink in our armour. For me it was rebellion and I have a feeling that the only way I was going to learn my lesson was through something I would never forget! It also showed me how my wrong reactions, when I react in my soul instead of my spirit, can have such far-reaching effects!

Our wonderful Lord Jesus uses everything that happens to us, the circumstances and the people, especially the people we live with, for good in our lives. We all know the verse, *'All things work together for good to those who love God'* (Romans 8:28), but that is only part of the verse. It continues: *'to those who are the called according to His purpose.'* But what is that purpose? The following verse shows us *'whom He foreknew, He also predestined to be conformed to the image of His Son . . .'* So that is what the Lord was doing in my life – making me more like Him – and that is what He wants to do in all our lives if we will let Him. Our husbands (or wives, parents, bosses, work-mates, etc.) are not our enemies and we must not fight against them.

'For we do not wrestle against flesh and blood, but against principalities, against powers, against the rulers of the darkness of this age, against spiritual hosts of wickedness in the heavenly places.' (Ephesians 6:12)

It is satan and all his cohorts who are our enemies.

By reacting negatively to the things that are happening in our lives, we are resisting God's work in us and prolonging the breaking process, the 'dying to self' that has to happen before we can be like Jesus, and also, before we will be really happy. Whatever we are going through, although the Lord is not necessarily causing it, He is allowing it for that specific purpose of making us like Jesus. Instead of resisting it, we should thank Him for it. Too many times I have reacted negatively to the daily trials of life. Because I have not accepted that Jesus is allowing them for a purpose and thanked Him for the situations and His working in me, I have had to go through the same kind of things over and over again. If I do not allow Jesus to change me through a situation, in His love He continues to work on that area of my life until, whatever it is that upsets or irritates me, does not upset or irritate me anymore.

For example, I was a very impatient person and could not bear to wait for people. It was such a waste of time and I had far better things to do than stand on a street corner waiting for somebody who did not turn up on time! The Lord had to allow me to be kept waiting so many times, until I learnt, not only to thank Him for the delay but also to **use** it by spending the time praying or worshipping Him. I had to learn not to get agitated but to stay in a rest and enjoy the opportunity to tell Jesus I love Him. That, of course, is only a small thing. There are much bigger issues that the Lord Jesus allows to arise in our lives, all of which can change us, draw us closer to Him and make us more like Him, or cause us to get upset and separate us from Him, depending on how we react. James 1:2–4 says,

> *'My brethren, count it all joy when you fall into various trials, knowing that the testing of your faith produces patience. But let patience have its perfect work, that you may be perfect and complete, lacking nothing.'*

J.B. Phillips' translation of verse 2 says,

> *'When all kinds of trials and temptations crowd into your lives, do not resent them as intruders, but **welcome them as friends**.'*

Jesus loves us exactly as we are – but He loves us too much to let us stay that way! When we fully realise that Jesus loves us and only allows these things to happen for our good, then we will truly be able to praise and thank Him for them and He can conform us to His image.

So we can react in our spirit, or we can react in our soul. Too often we react in our emotions – getting angry or feeling rejected etc. What Jesus wants us to do, and enables us to do if we avail ourselves of His grace, is to react in our spirit, by thanking Him and praising Him.

How does this work in practice? If somebody disagrees with us and tells us we are wrong we immediately have a choice. If we react in our soul, we will either get angry and argue, or we can resist that option but retreat into ourselves and feel rejected. If we react in our spirit, the Lord Jesus will enable us to calmly say 'I'm sorry' while inwardly saying, 'Thank You, Jesus. Bless them, Lord. I forgive them, in the Name of Jesus.' Of course, it gets more difficult if the other person is really intent on arguing and continues to be angry with us. All we can do, by God's grace, is to remain calm and say something like, 'I'm sorry I've upset you but I'm not going to argue with you because I love you!' And then change the conversation! Not only will that diffuse the situation, but it will enable us to stay in that wonderful close relationship with Jesus.

Chapter 12

Sowing to the Flesh

Another hindrance to maintaining our intimate love relationship with Jesus concerns our sowing,

> '...for whatever a man sows, that he will also reap. For he who sows to the flesh will of the flesh reap corruption, but he who sows to the Spirit will of the Spirit reap everlasting life.' (Galatians 6:7–8)

Sowing to the flesh is not necessarily sin. There are many things we can do which are not wrong in themselves but they do not help us. As Paul said,

> 'All things are lawful for me, but not all things are helpful; all things are lawful for me, but not all things edify.' (1 Corinthians 10:23)

Watching secular television is not wrong but what is it sowing to – the flesh or the Spirit? Watching the news is fine, but if you are anything like me, before we got rid of the television I would put it on for the news and very often it would stay on. I was very careful what programmes I watched, but even the most informative documentary was not sowing to the Spirit. I know this sounds very strong, but it was sowing to the flesh which reaps corruption! If you read David Wilkerson's book, *Set the Trumpet To Thy Mouth* (World Challenge, Inc.), you will find he is even stronger about television!

The newspaper is similar; reading the headlines and top stories may be alright but much of the rest is not necessary. You will say, 'We've got to know what's going on in the world!' And I agree with you but maybe if we cannot discipline ourselves to turn off the television or only read the front page of the newspaper, another option is the radio. In most countries there are fifteen-minute or half-hour news programmes at many times during the day and evening. What I do is listen to the news on the radio while I am preparing lunch or dinner and then I am not taking up time that I could spend with Jesus. This gives me the main stories without all the trivia and gory details that are not edifying. And strangely enough, I have never had any problem switching off the radio as soon as the news has finished. It does not have the same hypnotic effect that the television has! When we had a television I would sometimes watch a film which did not finish till very late and then I couldn't get up in the morning to have my quiet time with Jesus!

Reading secular books and magazines are not necessarily wrong either – but is it sowing to the flesh or to the Spirit? Going to the cinema is not necessarily a sin but Psalm 1:1 says we are blessed if we don't *'stand in the way of sinners or sit in the seat of the scornful,'* and certainly most of the films these days are definitely sinful! Even those films that Christians have recommended to me usually have some sex and/or violence in them and, for myself, I would rather not feed my spirit with that kind of thing.

Hobbies and pastimes are also not wrong and many of them can be used by the Lord, like gardening, photography etc. and it is good to have exercise by playing sports, but we must be careful how much of our time these things take up. It is a question of priorities. Are they robbing Jesus of the time we should be spending with Him? Do we feel edified, built up spiritually by them? Are they sowing to the flesh or to the Spirit?

Chapter 13

Busyness and Stress

A very subtle hindrance to our relationship with Jesus is when we get too busy and all of us, including ministers and missionaries, can get too busy. If we are too busy to spend time with Jesus we need to ask the Lord to show us what we can cut out of our busy schedules or how we can rearrange our schedules. For mothers of young children this can be a problem but even if you cannot spend much time reading your Bible in the mornings, or for a few minutes before falling asleep at night, you can still talk to Jesus during the day, when you are doing the washing or ironing, or stirring the soup. Those are the times you can tell Jesus how much you love Him. The devil will tell you you are too busy to have an intimate love relationship with Jesus but, as we know, he is a liar. And if you need a few minutes alone with Jesus, the bathroom is as good a place as any. Make sure you've got a good lock on the door so you are not disturbed!

For ministers and missionaries one of the biggest traps is when we get too busy working **for** Jesus that we do not have time to be **with** Him, sitting at His feet loving Him. David Wilkerson, in another of his books, *Hungry For More of Jesus* (Chosen Books), says,

> '[Jesus] is more interested in winning our whole hearts [for Himself] than in our winning the world for Him.'

He is after **you and me** – not our work for Him! We will never be able to maintain our love relationship with Jesus if we are too busy to stop and spend time with Him. This includes time reading the Bible for our own devotions, not just in order to prepare for a sermon, a Bible Study or a message for the Sunday School children.

When I am too busy I get too tired, and when I am too tired I can easily feel stressed. I start to think, 'Oh dear! I've not got enough time to do everything! I'll never be finished in time!' When I am stressed I stop being in a rest which means I am not trusting Jesus! I am not trusting Him to do whatever needs to be done or I'm blaming Him (or other people) for giving me too much to do! Either way, it is wrong and it is something that I personally had a battle with for many years until a friend told me that there was a spirit of stress. She prayed for me and after she cast it out in the Name of Jesus there has been a marked difference in my life. I still have to be on my guard against it but now that spirit of stress is only attacking from the outside and as soon as I recognise that I'm feeling stressed I can rebuke it in the Name of Jesus and it has to leave me alone. If I do not deal with the stress quickly it mars my relationship with Jesus. I get irritable and that mars my relationship with the people around me – especially my husband! Then it takes even longer to sort out the mess I have created and Jesus seems so far away. He has not moved – I have! I have moved from that place of childlike faith and trust that He is in control and that He *'worketh all things after the counsel of His own will'* (Ephesians 1:11, KJV).

It is true that there are times when it does seem there is too much to do, through no fault of our own and most of it cannot be done until the last minute, for example, before travelling and being away from home for several weeks. How can we avoid being stressed and coming out of that place of rest in Jesus? I have to be honest and say that although I'm very much better than I used to be, I'm still working on that one. But I do know that it is possible – I can't imagine Jesus getting stressed even when He suddenly had five thousand extra mouths to feed! And we have Jesus living within us. Somehow we must keep giving Him the burden of the work, asking Him to help us, and every time we start feeling stressed, rebuking the evil spirit and getting back into a rest again. I have found a wonderful promise in Proverbs 16:3 that has helped me time and time again:

> *'Commit your works to the Lord and your thoughts will be established.'*

When I mix that verse with faith and commit my works and all that has to be done to Jesus, I **know** that He will show me exactly what to do, when and how. And He does!

Chapter 14
Complacency

This too is a very subtle hindrance to our relationship with Jesus as we usually do not realise when we are becoming complacent until it seems that He is so far away and we begin to wonder why. When we first become Christians we are aware that we need the Lord's help with everything. If we are asked to give our testimony in church or to witness to somebody about Jesus we get very nervous and pray desperately that He will help us. After we have been doing these things for a while we think we know what to do and say, and perhaps begin to think we don't need the Lord's help anymore. We can do it by ourselves! We forget that without Him we can do nothing (John 15:5). Maybe at first it seems to be alright but after a while it feels dry and people don't respond the way they used to. It is because it is the Lord's **anointing** that breaks the yoke (Isaiah 10:27) and sets people free.

Many ministries have started off being really anointed but as soon as everything is going really well, very slowly and subtly there seems to be something missing. The anointing isn't on the work anymore. Why is this? Is it because the devil is attacking? This could be the reason but not necessarily. Is it because the ministry was not from the Lord in the first place? Or is it because the people are doing something wrong? Many times it is because complacency has crept in. Everybody knows what they are doing and how to do it so there isn't that cry to the Lord for His help. Pride and self-righteousness are also very much akin to complacency.

If we feel that our relationship with Jesus is good and we are doing well; we don't have any big problems and everything is running smoothly, thinking 'I'm OK. I'm doing just fine as I am. I go to church every week and

I help with the Sunday School.' etc., that is when we need to be very careful:

> 'Therefore let him who thinks he stands take heed lest he fall.' (1 Corinthians 10:12)

Jesus says,

> 'Blessed are those who hunger and thirst for righteousness, for they shall be filled.' (Matthew 5:6)

If we are not hungry for more of Jesus, that is when we are in danger of becoming complacent. If we stop being hungry for Jesus we will stop seeking Him, and if we stop seeking Him we will not find Him because to find Him we must search for Him with all our hearts (Jeremiah 29:13). An integral part of a close relationship with Jesus is seeking Him. If we ever feel we are becoming complacent, we must ask Jesus to give us a new hunger for Him and for His Word.

I sometimes wonder if we will even make it to heaven if we are complacent! As we have seen before, Jesus used strong words when He said to the church in Laodicea:

> 'I know your works, that you are neither cold nor hot. I could wish you were cold or hot. So then, because you are lukewarm, and neither cold nor hot, I will vomit you out of My mouth.' (Revelation 3:15–16)

Some years ago when Doug and I were in England for a couple of months, we went to a meeting in London where Ed Miller was speaking. Dr Miller was involved in the Argentinean Revival in the 1950s and 60s as well as other revivals. When we entered that meeting we were immediately impressed by a spirit of repentance that quickly brought an awareness of Jesus' Presence. As people responded, opening up their hearts for the King of Glory to come in, in a fresh and deeper way, many were soon lying on the floor as the Power of God touched them. At one point during that meeting, while Doug was under the Power of God, he had a vision. In the vision he had died and found himself knocking on one of the gates of heaven. An angel opened the door, looked at him, and shut it again.

'Hey! Just a minute! Let me in!' shouted Doug, but the door remained closed. He went to another door and knocked again. Another angel opened it, looked at him, and began to close it. 'Just a minute! Let me in!' Doug shouted again.

'What's your name?' the angel asked.

'Douggie Reed.'

'Sorry. You can't come in.'

'But my name's written in the Lamb's Book of Life.'

'Sorry. It's not written here.'

'But you've not looked. You've not had time to check.'

'What did you say your name was?'

'Douggie Reed! It's been in the Book for over 40 years! Please let me in!'

'No. I'm sorry. Douggie Reed can't come in. Only the Life of Jesus comes in here.'

The door was about to close when Doug shouted, 'It's no longer I that live, but Christ that lives in me' (Gal. 2:20).

The door opened wide and he was welcomed!

That's when Doug 'woke up" leaving him with the vivid realization that spiritually 'Douggie Reed' had to die. The only thing to be admitted into heaven was the **Life of Jesus**! On checking up in Revelation 2:17 (NIV), it says,

> *'To him who overcomes, I will give some of the hidden manna. I will also give him a white stone with a **new name** written on it, known only to him who receives it.'*

Revelation 3:12 (NIV) says,

> *'I will write on him **the name of My God** and the name of the city of My God, the new Jerusalem ... and I will also write on him **My new Name**.'*

I'm sure you will agree with me when I say that I don't think complacency is part of the Life of Jesus!

Chapter 15

Unbelief

One final thing that I would like to look at which hinders our relationship with Jesus is unbelief. Simply put, that means we do not believe something that Jesus has told us, either through His Word, through other people, or directly into our thoughts.

There is a very well-known and frequently used Bible verse that I think is wrongly, and sometimes misleadingly, translated in English.

> *'For God so loved the world that He gave His only begotten Son, that whoever believes in Him should not perish but have everlasting life.'* (John 3:16)

Evangelists often use this verse to say, 'you only have to believe....' But is this correct? My Bible tells me *'the devils also believe, and tremble'* (James 2:19), and I am sure the devils are not on their way to heaven!

How, then, should John 3:16 be translated? In the Greek, the word used for 'believe' actually means 'adhere to, trust, rely on'. It would therefore be much more correct, and closer to the consistent message throughout the Bible, to say and to preach, *'...whoever adheres to, trusts and relies on Him [the Lord Jesus Christ], should not perish but have everlasting life'*.

If we look at 1 Peter 2:7–8 in the King James Version, it is quite clear that the opposite of believe is disobey:

> *'Unto you therefore which **believe** He [Jesus] is precious: but unto them which be **disobedient**, the Stone which the builders disallowed, the same is made the Head of the corner, and a Stone of stumbling, and a Rock of offence,*

*even to them which stumble at the Word, being **disobedient . . .** '*

It follows, therefore, that to be ready to meet Jesus when we die or when He returns for His Bride, we need more than just a mental assent that Jesus is the Son of God. Our believing must contain something far deeper than that, which causes us to want to **obey** Him. Believing is something that is active, not passive. If we believe that a particular chair is safe to sit on and will not collapse under our weight, we will sit on it. If we refuse to sit on that chair it means we do not believe it is safe! To 'adhere to, trust and rely on' is much more active than just believing in a passive way. James is quite emphatic that *'faith without works is dead'* (2:20, 26), and says, *'I will show you my faith by my works'* (2:18). So faith, or believing, is active. It means we obey Jesus. We obey His written commandments and we obey Him when He speaks to us in our thoughts in that 'still small voice'.

First of all we must believe that it is Jesus speaking to us because He said

'My sheep hear My voice, and I know them, and they follow Me.'   (John 10:27)

Then, by mixing it with faith, we must act on what He is telling us. When we have a thought 'telephone such and such a person' we have three choices: obey immediately, put it off till later, or ignore it. I have invariably found that if I choose the first option I have rung that person at exactly the right time to help or encourage them in some way. The other person is blessed and I come off the 'phone also feeling blessed because I have helped somebody. May I encourage you – the next time you get a thought 'Telephone so-and-so,' or 'Write to such-and-such a person,' believe it is the Lord Jesus prompting you to do it and act on it! You will be blessed! If we choose either of the other two options we might not be aware that we have disobeyed the Lord until we notice a shadow in our relationship with Him. We also will not know the joy that obedience brings, and the strengthening of our faith that it brings too. We are much more likely to obey the next time we get the thought 'call so and so.' I have found for myself that the more I obey Jesus in the smaller things, the easier it is to obey Him in the bigger issues. I am beginning to know the voice of Jesus more clearly without thinking, 'Is that You speaking to me, Lord, or is it just myself?' By believing it is Jesus, it helps me to obey Him, and it keeps me in close communion with Him.

> *'If you keep My commandments, you will abide in My love.'*　　　　　　　　　　　　　　　(John 15:10)

Believing also brings us into a rest. Hebrews chapters 3 and 4 shows this very clearly.

> *'We who have believed do enter that rest.'*
> 　　　　　　　　　　　　　　　　(Hebrews 4:3)

and

> *' ... they could not enter in because of unbelief.'*
> 　　　　　　　　　　　　　　　　(Hebrews 3:19)

It is interesting that 4:6 says, *' ... did not enter* [into a rest] *because of disobedience.'* If we believe that Jesus is in control of a situation or that it is He who is telling us to do something, we do not need to worry about it. We can 'enter into a rest' – we can be at peace inside, even though all around us there is a storm, or the thing He is asking us to do seems too difficult.

Recently, however, the Lord Jesus has been showing me that in an intimate relationship with Him and a life of faith, He wants more than me just believing He is in control, believing I am in His will, or believing I am doing what He has told me to do. When I hear some people say 'I **believe** I'm doing what God wants,' I immediately

116

know that they are not so sure! On the other hand, when they say, 'I **know** I'm doing what God wants,' there is more confidence in their voices. How often, though, those same words are followed by a 'but'! 'I know I'm doing what God wants – but it's very difficult,' or 'I know this is where the Lord wants me – but the church isn't as good as the last one I went to,' etc.

What the Lord has been showing me is that after believing comes knowing and after knowing comes **acceptance**! True and complete rest comes when I **accept** what is happening – not just as something I have got to grin and bear, but as being God's best for me. And I can only truly accept the situation when I **mix it with faith**! Then I am able to say, for example, 'The fellowship I had when I was in that place was wonderful. And (not 'but'), although I don't have that same fellowship where I am now, it is equally wonderful because it's God's plan for me. He knows best and He's doing a work in my life.' That is when I can truly relax and enjoy where I am and who I am with and what I am doing – and receive all that the Lord Jesus has for me in that situation. And that is when I can truly worship Jesus with all my heart and know His Presence.

I am not saying we should sit back passively and accept anything the **devil** throws at us. It is not those things we must accept. It is the things we **know** are from the Lord that we should accept. During the end times we need to already have such an intimate relationship with Jesus and already be living a life of faith that we know what He is saying to us and what He is telling us to do, even if it means more difficulties or persecution. We will not be afraid of the outcome of obeying the Lord but we will be strong in faith like Daniel when he disobeyed king Darius' decree and continued praying to God like he always did, even though he knew it would mean being thrown into the lions' den. Like Peter in Acts 5:29, Daniel knew *'we ought to obey God rather than men.'* Daniel's faith and obedience did not stop him from being thrown into the lions' den, but it did stop the lions' mouths and when he was taken out of the den, *'no injury was found on him, because he believed in his God'* (Daniel 6:23). This not only meant Daniel was not harmed, but his God was so much glorified that the king made another decree

'[that everybody] *must tremble and fear before the God of Daniel.*
For He is the living God,
And steadfast forever;
His kingdom is the one that shall not be destroyed,
And His dominion shall endure to the end.
He delivers and rescues,
And He works signs and wonders
In heaven and on earth . . .' (Daniel 6:26–27)

We glorify our wonderful Lord Jesus and show forth His faithfulness when we obey Him – because we have believed, trusted, relied upon and adhered to Him in the midst of difficulties. If there is unbelief in our hearts we cast doubt on God's faithfulness to help and deliver us, and also our relationship with Him suffers drastically. In the episode I described concerning the computer in the chapter on wrong reactions, it was not just my resentment and rebellion that separated me from Jesus, but also my unbelief in not trusting that Jesus would help me and give me the ability and grace to use the computer. After the Lord had dealt with me and I had accepted the computer as being from Him, then he could help me with it. Now I wonder how I managed without it, especially in writing this book! Wonderful Jesus!

PART FOUR

Living By Faith

Chapter 16

Living By Faith

As we have already seen, if we love Jesus we will want to please Him. God's Word declares that

> '...without **faith** it is impossible to please Him.'
>
> (Hebrews 11:6)

and also

> '...the just shall live **by faith;**
> But if anyone draws back [from living by faith],
> My soul has no pleasure in him.'   (Hebrews 10:38)

Living by faith not only pleases the Lord but it is counted as being righteous before God as we can see from Abraham's life. God told him he was going to have a son, even though he was an old man,

> 'And he believed in the Lord, and He accounted it to him for righteousness.'   (Genesis 15:6 & Galatians 3:6)

In Romans 4:5 it says, 'his faith is accounted for righteousness' and in verse 9, 'faith was reckoned to Abraham for righteousness' (KJV). From this we see that God declares Abraham to be righteous because he believed and had faith in His Word. When it says, 'the just shall live by faith' (Habakkuk 2:4; Romans 1:17; Galatians 3:11 and Hebrews 10:38), what it really means is that to be just or righteous we must live by faith. Or, putting it another way, the only way for God to look at us as being righteous is to live by faith! That means trusting Jesus in every area of living. Most people use this expression 'living by faith' to refer to trusting the Lord for money because they do not have a salary-paying job, but it involves far more than this. It was not money that Abraham believed God for – he was a very rich man (Genesis 13:1).

First and foremost we have to accept **by faith**, that it is not what we do that makes us righteous. It is not keeping all God's commandments that makes us righteous although, as we have already seen, we will **want** to keep His commandments because we love Him and want to please Him. The Apostle Paul said he wanted to

'...be found in [Christ], *not having my own righteousness, which is from the law* [by keeping all the commandments], *but that which is through faith in Christ, the righteousness which is from God by faith.'*

(Philippians 3:9)

He also said

*'Of Him you are in Christ Jesus, who became for us wisdom from God – and **righteousness** and sanctification and redemption.'*   (1 Corinthians 1:30)

That means that Jesus Himself is our righteousness – and He is everything else too!

So living by faith does not mean only those who trust the Lord for finances, because that would rule out a lot of godly people. Hebrews chapter 11 is a chronicle of Old Testament saints

'Who through faith subdued kingdoms, worked righteousness, obtained promises, stopped the mouths of lions, quenched the violence of fire, escaped the edge of the sword, out of weakness were made strong, became valiant in battle, turned to flight the armies of the aliens [etc., etc.].'*   (Hebrews 11:33–34)

It is interesting that money is not mentioned even once! Living by faith means in **every** area of our lives. For example, when we first get saved it is through faith (Ephesians 2:8). When some people ask Jesus to forgive their sins, to come into their hearts and to take control of their lives they have a wonderful sense of peace or joy, but many others do not feel anything. They must accept that Jesus has actually done what they have asked **by faith**.

Doug and I lived in Israel for a number of years by faith and we now live in Hong Kong by faith. That is, we believe this is where the Lord has told us to live at this time, and that He will show us if and when it is time for us to go elsewhere. We have travelled and ministered in other countries by faith, believing that the Lord told us to go and that He would give us His words to speak in the churches to which He led us. In everything we do we must have faith that Jesus is leading us by His Spirit to be in the right place at the right time, speaking the right words to the right people – and that He will also provide the necessities to do this. This includes the strength, the ability, the anointing, the grace, the wisdom **and** the finances. Money is only a very small part of what we need faith for.

I am writing this book **by faith**. That is, I heard the Lord Jesus tell me to write it, through words He spoke to my heart, confirmed in numerous scriptures from my normal daily Bible readings, and the positive witness of the 'multitude of counsellors', and I have mixed that with faith and acted on it. I also have to have faith that the Lord will give me the exact words to write and that He will use it for His purposes.

When we read God's promises in the Bible the only way to appropriate them and have them become real in our lives is to **mix them with faith**. If we do not mix God's Word with faith it will not benefit us, as the writer to the Hebrews says in chapter 4:2:

'...*the word preached did not profit them, not being* **mixed with faith** *in them that heard it.*'

To mix it with faith means we **choose** to believe it. Believing is a choice, an act of will. How often do we hear people say something like this: 'If such and such happens, I'll believe.'? That means that if it does not happen they will not believe. They refuse to believe. They **will** not! If we can will **not** to believe then we can certainly will **to** believe!

I know that living by faith is the way the Lord Jesus wants us to live here and now. I also know that the more we get used to living this way now, the easier it will be for us in the end times because it has already become the 'norm' for us. In fact, if we do not know how to live by faith in the living God now, I think things will be much more difficult for us later when things get tough. As it says in Jeremiah 12:5,

> *'If you have raced with men on foot and they have worn you out, how can you compete with horses? If you stumble in safe country, how will you manage in the thickets by the Jordan?'*

So how do we live by faith? In simple terms it means that whatever the Lord says to us, we mix it with faith and choose to believe it. This applies to all the general promises He has made to all of us, as recorded in the Bible, and also to the specific words of exhortation, comfort and guidance that He gives to each of us as individuals in specific situations, either through His Word, through other people or as the Holy Spirit speaks directly to us in our thoughts.

At this point some people might say they do not have enough faith. My Bible tells me that

> *'God hath dealt to **every** man **the** measure of faith.'*
> (Romans 12:3c, KJV)

Apart from that, living by faith is not dependent on our faith so much as knowing that Jesus is **faithful**. It is not our faith, it is His **faithfulness**. Hallelujah! And the wonderful thing about it is that Jesus never asks us to do something that He Himself does not want to do through us.

'He who calls you is faithful, who also will do it.'
(1 Thessalonians 5:24)

I would now like to give you some examples of mixing God's promises with faith and also some of the times He has guided me by His Word both written and spoken.

Chapter 17

Household Salvation

When I first came to know Jesus I began praying for my family because I love them and want them to go to heaven when they die;

> 'For the wages of sin is death, but the gift of God is eternal life in Jesus Christ our Lord.'   (Romans 6:23)

Not only that, I want them to experience the peace and joy that I have had since I asked Jesus to take control of my life;

> 'Peace I leave with you, My peace I give to you; not as the world gives do I give to you. Let not your heart be troubled, neither let it be afraid.'   (John 14:27)

More recently I have also been concerned about how my loved ones will cope with the difficulties they may have to face during the Tribulation. Not only do I want to be ready myself, but I want them to be ready too.

Everybody who knows Jesus wants their family to know Him too. Everywhere we go people are always asking us to pray for their families: 'Please pray that my father gets saved.' 'Please pray for my mother. She doesn't know Jesus.' 'My sister is so unhappy. Please pray she'll become a Christian.' etc., etc. Because I know that everybody reading this wants their family to be saved and so that you do not have to keep worrying about them, I would like to share with you how to receive their salvation – **in your spirit**, by faith. There are many instances in the Bible that demonstrate that Jesus came to save whole households. For example, from the Old Testament:

1. **Noah and his family**. Although it was only Noah who *'found grace in the eyes of the Lord ... a just man*

and perfect in his generations' (Genesis 6:8–9), God saved all his family from the flood that destroyed the whole earth.

> *'Then the Lord said to Noah, "Come into the ark, you **and all your household**, because I have seen that you are righteous before Me in this generation."'*
>
> (Genesis 7:1)

2. **Lot and his family**. Sodom, the city where Lot lived, was very wicked and the Lord decided to destroy it. It was only *'righteous Lot, who was oppressed by the filthy conduct of the wicked'* (2 Peter 2:7), but the Lord gave his whole family the opportunity to escape and sent two angels to help them;

> *'Then the men* [angels] *said to Lot, "Have you anyone else here? **Son-in-law, your sons, your daughters, and whomever you have** in the city – take them out of this place! For we will destroy this place, because the outcry against them has grown great before the face of the Lord, and the Lord has sent us to destroy it."'*
>
> (Genesis 19:12–13)

It is true that Lot's sons-in-law refused to leave Sodom (v. 14) but his two daughters and his wife went with Lot, (v. 15–16). Later, his wife found the pull of the world too great for her, disobeyed the angels' instructions not to look back (v. 17) and became a pillar of salt (v. 26). From this we can see that our families are **not automatically** saved because of our relationship with Jesus. They still have to make their own decision, but I believe we can ask and receive their salvation **by faith** (John 16:24) because we know it is the Lord's will for them.

3. **Rahab and her family**. The children of Israel had gone through the wilderness and were preparing to cross the River Jordan and enter the promised land of Canaan. After Moses died, Joshua took over the

leadership and he sent two men to spy out the city of Jericho. They stopped at the house of a woman called Rahab. When the king of Jericho heard that spies had come, he sent his men to capture them but Rahab hid the spies and protected them. Later, when the danger was over, she said she knew that the Israelites' God was the true God and had given them the land (Joshua 2:9–11). In return for having protected them she then asked the spies to save her and her family:

> ' "Now therefore, I beg you, swear to me by the Lord, since I have shown you kindness, that you also will show kindness to my father's house ... and spare my father, my mother, my brothers, my sisters, and all that they have, and deliver our lives from death." '
>
> (Joshua 2:12–13)

The spies promised to save them but

> ' ... said to her: "We will be blameless of this oath of yours which you have made us swear, unless, when we come into the land, you bind this line of scarlet cord [representing the Blood of Jesus] in the window through which you let us down, and unless you bring **your father, your mother, your brothers, and all your father's household** to your own home. So it shall be that whoever goes outside the doors of your house into the street, his blood shall be on his own head, and we will be guiltless. And whoever is with you in the house, his blood shall be on our head if a hand is laid on him." '
>
> (Joshua 2:17–19)

Again we see that through one woman's faith in the true God, provision was made for her whole family to be saved. (This does not mean we have to have all the family living with us. The only reason Rahab's family had to go into her home was because there was going to be a battle.)

4. **Man of Bethel and his family**. After the Israelites had come into the promised land they still had many battles to fight against the wicked inhabitants.

> *'So the house of Joseph sent men to spy out Bethel ...*
> *and when the spies saw a man coming out of the city,*
> *they said to him, "Please show us the* [secret] *entrance*
> *to the city, and we will show you mercy." So he showed*
> *them the entrance to the city, and they struck the city*
> *with the edge of the sword; but they let the man **and***
> ***all his family** go.'*   (Judges 1:23–25)

Because of one man's act, all his family was saved.

Similar promises of our whole household to be saved are found in the New Testament:

1. **Cornelius and his family**. Cornelius was a centurion in the Roman army, not Jewish but *'a devout man and one who feared God'* (Acts 10:2). One day when he was praying, an angel

> *'...said to him, "Send men to Joppa, and call for*
> *Simon whose surname is Peter, who will tell you words*
> *by which you **and all your household** will be*
> *saved."'*   (Acts 11:13–14)

2. **Lydia and her family**. When Paul and Luke and others were preaching about Jesus in Philippi,

> *'...a certain woman named Lydia heard us.... The*
> *Lord opened her heart to heed the things spoken by*
> *Paul. And when she **and her household** were*
> *baptised...'*   (Acts 16:14–15)

At first only Lydia believed, but through her, all her family believed and were baptised.

3. **The Macedonian jailer and his family**. Paul and Silas were arrested and put in prison for preaching the gospel. When they prayed and sang hymns to God in the middle of the night, there was an earthquake and *'all the* [prison] *doors were opened and*

everyone's chains were loosed' (Acts 16:26). The jailer was afraid that all the prisoners had escaped and Paul had to stop him from killing himself (vs. 27–28). The jailer

> ' . . . *fell down trembling before Paul and Silas . . . and said, "Sirs, what must I do to be saved?" So they said, "Believe on the Lord Jesus Christ, and you will be saved, you* **and your household**.*"'*

(Acts 16:29–31).

Later, *'he* **and all his family** *were baptised'* (v. 33).

Although it is good to know all these scriptures, knowing them is not enough. They must be **mixed with faith**. All the promises in the Bible only become ours as we believe them. So too, if we want all our family to be saved we must believe the Lord's promises concerning them. We can pray something like this:

> 'Lord Jesus, thank you for saving me. You promised in Your Word that I and all my family should be saved. My mother [or brother or aunt or whoever you are particularly praying for] is part of my family, so I am claiming that promise for her [him]. Thank You for revealing Yourself to her [him]. In Jesus Name, Amen.'

As we pray we must **believe** it. It is no good thinking, 'Oh, my sister (or brother or niece or nephew) could never get saved. She's too bad (or too content with her life). She'll never see her need for Jesus.' If that is how we feel it means we do not love them, because *'love believes all things'* (1 Corinthians 13:7). And we should not pray for somebody if we cannot believe what we are praying for, because *'whatever is not from faith is sin'* (Romans 14:23).

Many people pray, 'If it be Your will, Lord . . . ' From all the Bible passages I have just quoted, it is obviously God's will for our families to be saved. If we know it is His will, then we can believe that He will answer our prayers:

> 'Now this is the confidence that we have in Him, that if we ask anything according to His will, He hears us. And if we know that He hears us, whatever we ask, we know that we have the petitions that we have asked of Him.'
>
> (1 John 5:14–15)

Hallelujah!

At the beginning of this chapter I said that we can receive our families' salvation in our spirit. How can we know we've received it if we cannot see it? Mark 11:24 says,

> 'Whatever things you ask when you pray, **believe** that you receive them, and you will have them.'

Also, in John 16:24 it says,

> 'Ask, and you will receive, that your **joy** may be full.'

For me, there was a certain point when I was praying for members of my family that I suddenly had the inward knowing that it was done, and with that knowing came such **joy**! When we receive something we have been asking for, we have joy. In prayer, when we suddenly have a joy it is because we know we have received what we have been asking for. We must keep on praying until we get that joy. Some people call this 'praying through'. That means, praying until we **know** our prayer is answered. The joy is the sign that we have received. One time when I was praying for my step-father, I received his salvation when I suddenly realised that although he was not in my original family, God had later brought him in to the family – not just to be a blessing to my mother, but **for his salvation**! That fact hit my spirit and I could not help but laugh out loud; I had such joy! Glory to Jesus! For each member of my immediate family I have had similar experiences at different times, and also for many of my extended family, as the Lord Jesus has burdened me to pray for them.

Now, when I pray for my family, I cannot pray for their salvation. That would indicate that I did not believe it was already done. In eternity there is no time, so in the spirit I can believe it is done (past tense) even though the evidence of it is still in the future.

> *'Faith is the substance of things hoped for, the evidence of things **not** seen.'* (Hebrews 11:1)

When I think of my family now, I thank the Lord Jesus for their salvation and the work that He is doing in their lives. I can also bind anything He shows me that is hindering His work in their lives, and loose them to the Holy Spirit's wooing.

> *'Whatever you bind on earth will be bound in heaven, and whatever you loose on earth will be loosed in heaven.'* (Matthew 18:18)

By faith, you too can have all your family saved right now, as you mix God's promises with faith, receive their salvation in your spirit and thank the Lord for it.

Chapter 18

My God Shall Supply All Your Need

One of the promises in the Bible that all of us need to mix with faith is,

> *'My God shall supply all your need according to His riches in glory by Christ Jesus.'* (Philippians 4:19)

Another promise is:

> *'Do not worry about your life, what you will eat or what you will drink; nor about your body, what you will put on ... but seek first the kingdom of God and His righteousness, and all these things shall be added to you.'*
> (Matthew 6:25–33)

This is a conditional promise – for the Lord to provide the things we need we must first be seeking His kingdom and His righteousness. A similar verse is:

> *'Oh, fear the Lord, you His saints!*
> *There is no want to those who fear Him.*
> *The young lions do lack and suffer hunger;*
> *But those who seek the Lord shall not lack any good*
> *   thing.'* (Psalm 34:9–10)

And again:

> *'No good thing will He withhold*
> *From those who walk uprightly.'* (Psalm 84:11c)

There are other conditions attached to this last promise; it means that if we do not receive the thing we are asking the Lord for, either it is not a **good** thing for us, or not a good thing for us at that time, or we are not walking uprightly.

Many years ago when I was living in Israel working for a tour company, there was a very difficult situation with one of the male tourists. He was drinking too much and causing problems for some of the others. Because he was a man I did not feel it was wise for me to deal with him and I felt it would be much easier if I was married and my husband could therefore deal with the problem. At that time I was 32 years old and the Lord had shown me that I would be getting married sometime but He had not yet brought the right one along. I had not been in any hurry to get married but now it seemed it would have solved a problem. As I was praying and asking Jesus why He hadn't brought my husband along yet, Psalm 84:11 came to my mind very clearly. My first response was to ask Him if I was not walking uprightly. He did not show me anything wrong so I had to assume that the thing (husband) I was asking the Lord for was not good for me at that time. I accepted that answer and then asked Jesus what I should do about the specific problem with the tourist. Very quickly the thought came to me that there was a brother in church that had an evangelistic ministry and he would be the ideal person to come along-side the tourist and talk with him. I believed that was the Lord speaking to me and mixed it with faith. The following day I talked to the church about the problem tourist and this evangelist brother immediately said he would go and talk to him. I told him which hotel he was staying in and he went there the next day, found the man, witnessed to him and led him to the Lord! As a result his drinking stopped and therefore he was no longer a problem to the other tourists – my God supplied my need, His way, not mine!

Missionary to China Hudson Taylor used to say, 'God's work done God's way will never lack God's supply.' As missionaries ourselves, Doug and I have often had to hang on to the Lord's promise that he will supply all our needs. When we first came to Hong Kong in 1984 we had a little money from the sale of our house in England but learning basic Cantonese at a language school, together with the rent, soon ate up all of that. As I saw our bank-balance go down I was excited to see how the Lord would provide, but it was not going to be as easy as previously, and for two years we were severely tested.

Although we never told anybody that we were running short of money, several people suggested that we teach English. At first the thought horrified me; I did not know how to teach! And I did not have the patience to be a teacher! That, of course, was one reason why the Lord did want me to teach – to teach **me** patience!

Rather than teaching English in a school, we sensed that Jesus wanted us to teach at home. As we were seeking the Lord about this, we felt He was saying that we should not charge for the lessons. This was certainly against our reasoning, especially as the whole purpose for us even thinking about teaching English was to earn some money to help pay the rent. But the Lord gave us two very clear scriptures which told us otherwise:

'*Freely you have received, freely give.*' (Matthew 10:8b)

and,

' *. . . present the gospel of Christ without charge.*'
(1 Corinthians 9:18)

When we shared this with the Chinese Christians we knew, they insisted that we would have to charge or people would think we were no good. As they knew their own people better than we did, we thought we should listen to them. We decided to compromise and just charge a very small amount.

We put a big board outside our home with the words, 'English Lessons – $25' and our telephone number. We knew that people in the city were charging over HK$50 at that time, so we thought $25 (approx. US$3) was very reasonable. I was quite surprised when I received a telephone call from a neighbour asking how long the course was.

'As long as you like,' I replied.

'For $25?'

'Oh, that's just for one hour.'

'Very expensive. Cannot do.'

'That's OK. Come anyway. No charge,' I said, remembering that that was what the Lord had originally told us. Inwardly I was saying, 'Forgive us, Lord, for listening to men and not to You. You always know best.'

A few days later the neighbour came for her first English lesson, bringing with her more than $25 in cookies and soft drinks! We changed the wording on the board outside the house to read, 'Free English Lessons,' and we were soon teaching classes of up to ten students four evenings a week and several hours during the daytime to individuals. Although that first student had not been able to afford the $25 an hour, there were others who could, and wanted to pay us, but we knew we must do what Jesus told us. We had to **mix His Word with faith**. Most of the students did, however, pay us in kind, bringing fruit, vegetables, chickens, pigeons, and eggs galore. Not only were we being fed, but we also had ample opportunity to get to know our neighbours and to talk to them about Jesus. We were often invited to their homes and they helped us with advice as we grew vegetables in our garden. The two evenings a week when we had the advanced English classes later developed into more of a Bible-study, and a few of the young people committed their lives to Jesus. Certainly, God's ways are higher than our ways (Isaiah 55:9), and certainly we always had food on the table, even if our diet was sometimes a little monotonous. We were given so many eggs and bananas that when we went to a mid-week Bible-study at a nearby English speaking church, we would sometimes take four or five dozen eggs and several bunches of bananas to give to the people there. Often, when we arrived home after the Bible-study, there would be another four or five dozen eggs and two or three hands of bananas sitting on our doorstep!

Although we praised the Lord for His provision of food, those two years were not easy as we often had to pay the rent by instalments, though we always managed to pay the full amount before the following month's rent was due. We thanked God for Eric, the young man we paid the rent to, who was a Christian and understood our situation but respected our wishes and did not tell other people that we had no money. At that time we were holding children's meetings in a nearby village, three afternoons a week. We did not have the bus-fare so we walked the twenty-five minutes there and back, even in the pouring rain. When our neighbours saw us walking and asked us why, we told them it was good exercise!

Despite the fact that we often received letters from friends on other mission-fields asking for money, we never felt this was what the Lord Jesus wanted us to do. We knew He wanted us to trust Him and Him alone. We knew He was fully aware of our needs – in fact, He knew them better than we did because He knew ahead of time what was going to happen. We knew, and had proved by experience, that our wonderful, faithful Lord Jesus is well able to talk to His people and tell them our needs without us telling them. And what a blessing it is for those who give when they know they have heard God's voice. We always endeavoured not to even hint at needing money because we did not want people to give to us because they felt they ought to, or out of the kindness of their hearts, but only because the Lord had told them to. We also did not want to stop the Lord doing His work in us. We wanted to live by faith in God alone. Yes, He usually uses people, but it is so often not the people we might expect to give. During those two years of testing we sent our newsletters to many people in England, America,

Australia, and several other countries around the world, but never once mentioned money or any needs, not even saying, 'We are trusting the Lord to supply the rent.' People say that this is not asking for money, but I feel it is still making it very obvious that they want people to send it!

But God **is** faithful, and though we were sorely tempted to do what everybody else did and let our needs be known, He did

> '... not allow [us] to be tempted beyond what [we were] able, but with the temptation also [made] the way of escape, that [we were] able to bear it.'
>
> (1 Corinthians 10:13)

Every now and again, one of our Chinese brothers or sisters would give us two or three hundred Hong Kong dollars and we would be able to finish paying the rent or pay the electricity bill.

Even though we had now decided we would not take money from our students, and had told them so, there was one occasion when we did. A young Chinese lady, River, had been staying with us for about a month while she studied for her school examinations because her own home was too noisy and crowded for her to concentrate. We had not charged her any rent because we knew she would not be able to pay it. On her next to last evening, while eating dinner with us, she said she would like to cook for us the following evening. I agreed and she said she would buy the meat and vegetables on her way home from school the next day, if I could provide the rice and cooking oil. That was fine for me, especially as it would give me a break from cooking. There was only one problem – I had just used the last of the rice and oil for dinner that night. We had no money to buy any more and we did not want to tell her. 'Please, Lord! We need some rice and oil, or the money to buy it,' I silently cried out to the Lord.

The following day I was excited to see how Jesus would supply the rice and oil. I did not have the bus-fare to go to town to collect our mail from the mailbox and it was too far to walk. I had no idea how deliverance could come but I knew the Deliverer. I expected River to arrive home at 6 o'clock and at ten minutes to six there was still no provision. Every time I was tempted to worry I said, 'Thank You, Lord, for what You are going to do. Thank You, Jesus, for Your provision.' At five minutes to six there was a ring on our front door-bell. When I opened the door I saw it was a neighbour whose daughter I taught English. She was holding a basket of eggs in one hand and waving two hundred-dollar bills with the other. As she handed them to me I took the basket of eggs and, thanking her, said I could not take the money. She was very insistent but I was equally as insistent that I could not take it, though I certainly wanted to! Suddenly she thrust one of the hundred dollar notes into my pocket and ran away. I protested but she had gone. Just then I looked up the path towards the main road and I saw River walking towards me. This was obviously the Lord's provision, and as so often is the case, just in the nick of time. 'Thank You, Jesus,' I whispered as I breathed a sigh of relief! God is never late, but He is not usually early either! As River walked in, I walked out to the village store and bought rice and oil.

At the end of this approximately two-year period, a young Chinese man came to us and said,

'Have you got any needs?'

'Jesus meets all our needs,' Doug replied.

'Yes, but I don't think you've got any money, and God's telling me to meet your needs. I'm not going to any church at the moment so I've got some tithe money. Tell me what you need and I'll give it to you.'

'If we had any needs we would only tell Jesus.'

'But I think Jesus wants you to tell me so I can help you,' the young man insisted.

'Well, if that's how you feel, go and ask Jesus what we need. If we have any needs, He knows what they are and He can tell you.'

'But Jesus doesn't talk to me. I can't hear His voice.'

'You're a sheep, aren't you? Jesus says His sheep hear His voice.'

'Yes, but ... .'

'Well, you go for a walk and ask Him if we have any needs, and if so, what they are. Here's a piece of paper so you can write down what He says to you. The first thought that comes into your head – you have to believe that is the Lord speaking to you. You have to mix it with faith. Your second thought will just be your reasoning. And if He doesn't say anything to you, don't give us anything!'

Doug waved him out of the front door and turned to me.

'What do we need, darling? Let's reckon up and write it on a piece of paper.'

We sat down and calculated what we needed at that time. (I cannot remember the exact figures so I have just made a rough estimate here. I trust the brother concerned will forgive me if it is not the same as he remembers it.) We still owed HK$1,200 on that month's rent and there was an electricity bill for $247 that needed to be paid before the end of the week. I wrote those down.

'If I could get that car outside tested and licensed, I could sell it,' Doug added. 'Then we'd have next month's rent, too!' Months before, he had bought this crashed car very cheaply at an auction. He had repaired it but had never had the money to get it on the road. Our neighbours saw we had a car and thought we were quite rich, though it puzzled them why we never used it!

'OK' I replied. 'What will that cost?'

'$1,240 for the licence and another $150 for the test.'

'Alright. And we've no bread left, or onions. I could do with another $5.20 for bread and I should be able to get an onion for 80 cents.' I jotted down a further $6.

We added it all up and wrote down the total: $2,843.

A few minutes later the young man came back.

'This is ridiculous!' he exclaimed, handing us his piece of paper. 'Look what my first thought was. $2,843!'

Smiling, we showed him what we had written down on our piece of paper. 'See! You **can** hear God's voice. That's exactly what we need. Praise the Lord!'

Totally amazed that Jesus had spoken to him, the young man gave us the money. Several minutes later he went on his way, still shaking his head and mumbling, 'I can't believe it! I can't believe it!'

A few days later Doug was able to license and sell the car. He bought two more scrap cars, repaired them and then sold them.

That was the end of that period of financial testing, but certainly not the end of the Lord's supplying all our needs. Almost everyday He demonstrates that He is our Provider, sometimes in big ways and sometimes in not so big, but equally wonderful ways. So many times the Lord has laid it on different people's hearts to send us money or to give us food, clothes, furniture and other things. This has meant that we can use the money we do have on rent or travel etc.

How the Lord provided for us to have my first book printed was quite remarkable. I originally wrote it in 1983–4 when we were still living in Israel. Very few people knew I had written the book and it was not accepted by any of the publishers I sent it to. It literally got put on the shelf for several years until, in 1990, I felt the Lord telling me to go through it, change the way it was written and add a few other things. At that time He also told me not to sell the book but to give it away. As I was praying one day, specifically asking the Lord what He wanted me to do with the book, He suddenly reminded me of a Bible verse I had read that morning. Proverbs 23:23 said,

*'Buy the truth, and **do not sell it**.'*

Also in verse 4 of the same chapter,

'Labour not to be rich.' (KJV)

These verses came to my mind so forcibly and so unexpectedly that I knew it could not be my own idea. And it was not exactly what I had wanted to hear!

Not selling the book meant a publisher would not be interested in it and I had absolutely no idea how to go about getting it into print myself! But I mixed the word with faith and said, 'OK Lord. If that's what You want me to do, that's fine by me, but You'll have to show me how to go about it and also provide the funds.'

With that I committed it to the Lord and continued working on the manuscript. Two or three weeks later, a Chinese friend of ours came to Hong Kong to minister with a small group of Christians from England. Doug and I were fellowshipping with them one evening and I was sharing a little of what Jesus had done in my life. One of the group casually commented that I should write a book. Doug said that I had but it had not been accepted by a publisher. Another lady in the group turned to me and said,

'Send the book to us. My husband is a Christian publisher and we can look at it for you.'

'But the Lord has told me not to sell it, but to give it away,' I replied.

'OK. If that's what you feel.'

'But maybe you can tell me how I go about getting it into print. I've no idea.'

'That's no problem. We can do what they call a "production job". If you send it to us, we'll get it typeset and printed for you.'

'Oh, that's great. I've still got a little more work to do on it, but when I've finished I'll send it to you. How much do you think it will cost?'

'Well, of course that depends on the length of the book and the cover you have and many other things, but I suppose an average book of about 200 pages would cost about £3,000.'

'OK. Then I'll send you the manuscript when it's ready.'

I went home that night so excited. I knew meeting this lady was not a coincidence and getting the book into print was not going to be such a mammoth task after all. Because the Lord had supplied that need, I knew He would supply the money too.

Doug and I told **nobody** what Jesus had shown us to do but almost immediately we started receiving large sums of money in the mail. We had often received small amounts, but nothing like this. £300 came from a brother who used to live with us but had not had any money in those days. Now he wanted to pay us back what he felt he owed us. He had no idea how perfect the timing was! Another day we received £500 in £20 notes, in a brown envelope marked 'On His Majesty's Service'! To this day we still have no idea who sent it. All we know is that it was from Jesus!

Other amounts, large and small, came in so that by the time I sent the manuscript off to the publisher we had approximately £3,000! All that without having told anybody what we needed, except the Lord Jesus Himself. He certainly is Jehovah Jireh, our Provider. Hallelujah!

As I have said before, now is the time we must practise trusting the Lord Jesus to provide all our needs so that it will be the normal way of living for us in the days ahead if we have no other option; if we can neither buy nor sell without taking the 666 mark of the beast (Revelation 13:16–18). From v. 10 ('*the patience and the faith of the saints*') it does look like we are still here, doesn't it?

Chapter 19

Russia

In June 1991 Doug commented that a young Chinese pastor we knew, kept asking him, week after week, when we were next going to Israel. And week after week, Doug told him we were not thinking of going, but he still kept asking, until one day we thought, 'Maybe the Lord's trying to tell us something!' The next morning, before we read our daily Bible readings, we asked the Lord to show us if He wanted us to visit Israel. That day we read,

> 'Comfort, yes, comfort My people!' (Isaiah 40:1)

and,

> 'Say to the cities of Judah, Behold your God!'
> (Isaiah 40:9)

Two days later we read,

> 'You will arise and have mercy on Zion;
> For the time to favour her,
> Yes, the set time, has come.' (Psalm 102:13)

Then the following day,

> '...observe the Feast of Tabernacles...'
> (Deuteronomy 16:13)

All this was in our normal daily Bible-reading schedule, and that week our church memory verse was Acts 1:8,

> '...You shall be witnesses to Me in Jerusalem.'

This was a time when we had to choose what to do with what the Lord Jesus seemed to be saying to us. We could either mix these scriptures with faith and act on them, or we could choose to ignore them. We decided to do the former and go to Israel. It had been seven years since we had left and it looked like the Lord was telling us to go for the Feast of Tabernacles at the end of September. My stepfather had just died and we knew my mother wanted us to go to England to help her so we could combine the two. This was wonderfully confirmed a week or so later when we read Deuteronomy 31:10–11, which said,

> 'At the end of every seven years ... at the Feast of Tabernacles, when all Israel comes to appear before the Lord. ...'

Although we did not need any more confirmation than that, somebody who had no idea of our proposed trip then gave us the book about Lydia Prince, *Appointment in Jerusalem*!

After making enquiries at the travel agent we realised it would be much cheaper to go to Israel from England than to go direct from Hong Kong and we asked my mother to book those flights for us. The day we were going to the travel agent to book our flights to England, however, a verse from our Bible readings seemed to jump out at us:

> 'You shall not go out with haste, nor go by flight.'
> (Isaiah 52:12)

Although we knew that the context of this verse was talking about the Israelites fleeing from the country they were in, it seemed that the Lord was saying to us that we should not fly to England. This was very strange and we didn't understand it but we felt we better not go to the travel agent until we knew what the Lord was saying to us. Two days later another verse jumped out at us:

> 'They [Joseph and Mary] *departed for their own country another way.'* (Matthew 2:12)

Doug had read it in the New International Version which was even clearer:

144

*'They returned to their country by **another route**.'*

We were puzzled! 'But how else can we go, Lord? Ship will take us far too long and we can't go overland, can we?'

A few days after this Doug was going through a drawer full of maps and brochures on Hong Kong when he came across a flyer that had been given to us on the street months before. In amazement he read out the headlines to me:

'Trans-Siberian Express'!

So **that** was what the Lord wanted. He wanted us to go on the Trans-Siberian Express! But why would He want us to go through Russia? Wasn't that rather a long way round?

We were just trying to digest this bit of information when another friend, Maren (who also knew nothing about our proposed trip), telephoned us enthusing over a book she had just finished reading and felt very strongly that we should read. It was Steve Lightle's *Exodus 2*, about the Lord's plan to bring the Soviet Jews back to Israel. Although we had read it several years previously, it was now very timely re-reading. Was this why God wanted us to go through Russia? Were there some Jewish people the Lord wanted us to meet and tell them to go back to Israel?

Again we had a choice. We could either dismiss the whole idea as 'coincidence', or we could mix it with faith and trust that the Lord Jesus had a purpose for us going on the Trans-Siberian Express. We decided to mix it with faith and we left Hong Kong on 19 August. It took us two days on the train to get to Beijing where we were to pick up our Trans-Siberian rail tickets and Russian visas from the travel agency. Just before we arrived in Beijing we heard rumours that there had been a coup in Russia to try to overthrow President Gorbachev. When we got to our travel agent we found it was true and everybody was talking about it. Several young western students who were booked on the same train as us, were gathered in the office glued to the radio trying to find out more details. There were also lots of rumours that foreigners were getting attacked and travellers having their luggage stolen. Some of the students were cancelling their train bookings as their parents called and insisted they **fly** home using their credit cards.

'Lord!' we cried. 'We're really sure **You** told us to go this way so we're going to trust You to keep us safe. But what's going to happen to Gorbachev? Please give us an answer to people's questions.'

The next day's Bible readings included 1 Samuel 14, where King Saul was fighting the Philistines and vowed that any of his army that ate that day would die. His son Jonathan was busy fighting in a different place and, not having heard the vow, he ate some honey. When Saul found out about it he said that Jonathan must die, but the people argued for Jonathan who had won a great battle that day and *'so **the people rescued Jonathan**, and he did not die'* (v. 45). We felt this was a direct answer from the Lord concerning Gorbachev! He would be released, and we were to speak it out and proclaim it. Quite a number of the train travellers knew by this time that we were Christians and believed the Bible, and they were joking about our 'hot-line' to heaven. When we told them what the Lord had shown us they argued, 'Gorbachev will have been shot by now. Nobody will ever see him again!' We could fully understand why they said that but we mixed God's Word with faith and continued to *'hold fast the confession of our faith'* (Hebrews 10:23, KJV).

Although we knew that many Christians around the world would be praying for the situation in Russia, we also asked the Lord **why** Gorbachev should be released. He told us it was because he had enabled over 300,000 Jewish people to leave the Soviet Union and return to Israel. (Hundreds of thousands more have since returned but that was the approximate figure at the time.) The Lord would bless Gorbachev because he had blessed

Israel! The promise *'I will bless those who bless you'* in Genesis 12:3, 26:3–4, 27:29 and Numbers 24:9 is still valid today for everybody who blesses Israel. (The opposite is also still valid today: in Genesis 27:29 Isaac says to his son Jacob, who was later renamed Israel, *'Cursed be everyone who curses you.'* From the original Hebrew this should be translated 'cursed be everyone who despises, lightly esteems you [Israel].' In other words, it is in our best interests to respect, honour, bless and help Israel and the Jewish people if we want God's blessing on our lives. If we despise Israel or in any way mistreat the Jewish people, we could be incurring God's curse on our lives!)

Our fellow travellers were quite amazed when news came through that the people had indeed risen up to rescue Gorbachev and that he was free! It opened the way for us to talk to them a lot more about Jesus during the six days we were on the train to Moscow after we boarded it that night.

We were also on the look-out for any Jewish people and on the first morning of the journey two men walking along the corridor stopped to talk to us, asking us how we came to be on that train. We knew immediately that they were Jewish and asked them if they were on their way home.

'Home? We're from Brazil.'

'But you're Jewish, aren't you?'

'W-e-l-l, y-e-s,' one of the men reluctantly admitted. 'How do you know?'

'We just know. So if your Jewish your home is Israel, isn't it? That's one of the reasons we're on this train – to tell the Jewish people to go back to Israel!'

'Just a minute! Don't go away! We want to go and get our friends to hear your story.'

With that they hurried off down the corridor, reappearing five minutes later with two other men carrying video cameras and microphones. It was a film crew! The second two men were Italian and also Jewish! They were making a documentary on the Trans-Siberian Express and they filmed us as we answered their questions. We told them how God had shown us to do this trip, by reading His Instruction Book. These were intelligent, open-minded men, who understood that God might just have a word for the viewers of their film, and they asked us if we could give them a 'message' from God the following day! 'Yes! With pleasure!'

The following morning we read them the scripture that says,

> ' "The days are coming," says the Lord, "that they shall no longer say, 'As the Lord lives who brought up the children of Israel from the land of Egypt,' but, 'As the Lord lives who brought up and led the descendants of the house of Israel from the north country and from all the countries where I had driven them.' And they shall dwell in their own land." '　　　　　　　　　　　(Jeremiah 23:7–8)

Through this we explained God's plan for the Jewish people, that He is calling them back to Israel, and that the Messiah's coming is getting nearer. (When the 'north country' or the 'land of the north' is mentioned in the Bible it is generally accepted as referring to Russia.)

Each day, for five days, these men came with their cameras and more questions. When they asked us what was going to happen to Russia and China, the Lord gave us the verse

> 'Righteousness exalts a nation,
> But sin is a reproach to any people.'　　(Proverbs 14:34)

It was an amazing opportunity! We were so excited, and amazed at the Lord's leading us to come this way and His timing!

At last the train pulled into the railway station in Moscow. We knew the Lord Jesus had more than just sight-seeing for us to do in the four days we would be there, but what? Each morning we asked the Lord to show us what He wanted us to do and where He wanted us to go. The first two days nothing spectacular happened but we believed, by faith, that we had done what was asked of us – and it really was interesting seeing Red Square, the guards outside Lenin's tomb, and a little of how the people lived – queuing up for ages to buy a loaf of bread, and riding on the buses and underground railway.

The third day was a Saturday, the Jewish Sabbath. We asked the Russian family we were staying with if they knew where there was a synagogue. They directed us to one not too far from their home. When we arrived the morning service was in progress so Doug quietly donned his yamulke (skull-cap) and joined the men downstairs while I put a scarf over my hair and went up to the ladies' balcony. I picked up a Hebrew prayer book, found where they were up to and prayed in tongues (see pages 63–66) until the service was over.

'OK Lord – who do you want me to speak to?'

Looking down over the balcony I saw Doug moving towards the bima (raised platform) where the rabbi stood. Later I found out he had talked to the rabbi who spoke a little English, and had shown him the Old Testament scriptures that talk about God's plan to bring the Jewish people back to Israel from all the places they had been scattered, including Russia. He also showed him Jeremiah 16:16 which says,

> ' "Behold, I will send for many fishermen," says the Lord, "and they shall fish for them; and afterward I will send for many hunters, and they shall hunt them from every mountain and every hill, and out of the holes of the rocks." '

(Also read Jeremiah 23:3–8; 30:3; 31:7–9; Ezekiel 39:25–29).

I greeted a few of the ladies but they did not seem to speak English or Hebrew, only Russian and Yiddish. I went downstairs to the lobby where many of the men were congregating. One of them responded with a big smile when I said 'Shalom' to him. (Shalom means peace in Hebrew and is a common greeting in Israel.) Encouraged by this I asked him if he spoke Hebrew or English and he replied in faltering Hebrew. As I told him that Doug and I used to live in Israel, and why we were now in Moscow, several others gathered round. Doug soon joined me and, with one of the men interpreting, we were able to show them through the Scriptures that God wanted them to go and live in Israel.

'Oh, but things are much better here now,' a few of them answered.

We reminded them that for many years it had been almost impossible to get an exit permit to leave any part of the Soviet Union (as it was then called), but now Mr Gorbachev was making it much easier.

'Yes, we know. But this is our home. We were born here and all our family and friends are here. It's not easy to leave everything behind and start again in a new country. What if we can't find work?'

'We know it's not easy,' we agreed, 'but if that's where God wants you, then it will be the best place for you. He'll help you. And things in Russia could get worse again overnight if there is another coup. The doors could shut anytime. You must think about it seriously before it's too late.'

We showed them the verse in Jeremiah 16:16 about the fishers and hunters and explained how God had sent us to 'fish' for them but if they did not take any notice, then He would have to send hunters and they might have to flee with only the clothes they stood up in.

'OK. We'll think about it,' they replied and they thanked us warmly for talking to them.

We left the synagogue with joy in our hearts, knowing we had done what the Lord had brought us to Moscow for, and praying for all those we had talked to. We then mixed another of God's promises with faith – in Isaiah 55:11 He says

> '[My Word] *shall not return to Me void,*
> *But it shall accomplish what I please,*
> *And it shall prosper in the thing for which I sent it.'*

Amen! So be it!

Chapter 20

The Philippines

Our first trip to the Philippines in April/May 1996 was by faith, every step of the way. It is quite a long story but I include it here because I want to illustrate how living by faith encompasses every area of our lives.

One of the Filipino domestic helpers in Hong Kong had read my book *What Do YOU Want, Lord?* and had given a copy to her pastor in Baguio, Luzon. After reading it, Pastor Joseph wrote to me asking for more copies of the book and then wrote several times during the following 2 or 3 years. In February 1996 we received a letter from him inviting us to speak at his group of churches' annual convention on 1st–3rd May. My first reaction was excitement as my spirit rose and when Doug read the letter it was obvious from his face that he felt the same. We had often said to each other that we would like to go to the Philippines sometime. Was this the Lord's time? We asked Jesus to show us through our normal daily Bible readings. There was nothing. Day after day there was nothing specific. We both **felt** it was right but we knew that our feelings could be misleading, so we really wanted two or three definite words from the Scriptures.

Shortly after that two friends, Iolo and Freda, came to visit us on their way to minister in a different part of the Philippines. We never said a word to them about our invitation to the Philippines, and prayed that if the Lord did want us to go, Iolo and Freda would say something to confirm it. And indirectly they did. It seemed that everything they said was about stepping out in faith. Freda told us a story about the first time she went to Spain. She did not have any definite scriptures from the Lord, although she had asked for them, but she really believed it was what the Lord wanted her to do despite very difficult circumstances. By faith she went, and from the things the Lord did, it was obviously right that she had gone. Hearing this and other things they said, made us wonder if the Lord was telling us to go to the Philippines without any confirming scriptures. We had always had plenty of Bible verses to confirm previous decisions we had made, especially major decisions. I had over thirty verses to confirm I was to marry Doug! The Bible says, *'in the mouth of two or three witnesses shall every word be established'* (Deuteronomy 19:15; Matthew 18:16; 2 Corinthians 13:1, KJV), and *'in the multitude of counsellors there is safety'* (Proverbs 11:14, 15:22, 24:6).

This time we got the impression that the Lord Jesus was stretching our faith. Everything we heard or read was telling us to step out in faith and accept the invitation. We had peace in our hearts as we wrote to Pastor Joseph saying yes.

Immediately after we had sent the letter an amazing thing happened. We started getting scriptures to confirm our decision! Every day, without really looking for them, they were jumping out of the Bible at us: *'Now is the accepted time'* (2 Corinthians 6:2c); *'...preached in His Name among all nations'* (Luke 24:47); *'preach the gospel in the regions beyond you'* (2 Corinthians 10:16), etc.

Also in Luke 24:28–32 was the story of the two disciples on the road to Emmaus. After they had invited Jesus in to eat with them, v. 31 says, *'their eyes were opened.'* It was as though the Lord Jesus was reminding us of an important principle: revelation comes **after** commitment! For many people, including myself, when we first ask Jesus into our lives and commit our lives to Him, we do not really understand what we are doing. It is only afterwards that the Holy Spirit reveals Jesus and His love to us.

After this more scriptures followed, reassuring us that Jesus was leading us and would equip us for the ministry ahead:

'I send an Angel before you to keep you in the way and to bring you into the place which I have prepared,'

(Exodus 23:20)

and

'I sent you to reap that for which you have not laboured ...' (John 4:38)

Around that time, I knew there was an International Women's Aglow convention on in Manila from 17th–20th April. Again my spirit rose so I felt the Lord was telling me to go to that too. The timing fitted in with Pastor Joseph's convention; Doug could join me after the Aglow convention and we could have nine or ten days rest together before going north to Baguio. Everything I read in the Bible encouraged me to step out in faith for this too. Doug agreed and we rang the travel agent who was arranging a special Cathay Pacific package deal for the flights and hotel for the other Aglow ladies. I explained that I would go with the other ladies on the 17th April but not return with them, and it was arranged that Doug would come and join me for the last night at the hotel. As I was booking our flights the travel agent asked me when we would be returning to Hong Kong and explained that it would be cheaper if it was within 21 days – an open ticket would be more expensive. I talked it over with Doug and we felt that 21 days would be sufficient. After the convention in Baguio we would still have time to spend a few extra days with them if they wanted us to. So we booked the return flight for 8th May, exactly 21 days after I was flying out.

The next few days we excitedly started preparing for the trip until we got a phone call from Pastor Joseph. He had received our letter and was very happy we were going but the dates for the convention had been changed. It was now going to be on 8th–10th May. Would that still be alright for us? My mind started racing. Our return flights were on 8th May – we would have to change them. Inwardly I questioned the Lord and felt He was saying, 'This thing is from Me.' I told Pastor Joseph we would go and we would telephone him a few days beforehand to tell him exactly what time we would arrive.

I came off the telephone and went straight for my Bible. It was still early in the morning and I had not read my readings yet. Doug was still sleeping.

'What's going on, Lord? Have we completely misheard You? Please show me!'

It was 30th March and I read:

'He is a shield to those who put their trust in Him.'
(Proverbs 30:5)

Then in Philippians chapter 4:

'So stand fast in the Lord.'   (verse 1)

'Be anxious for nothing, but in everything by prayer and supplication, with thanksgiving, let your requests be made known to God; and the peace of God, which surpasses all understanding, will guard your hearts and minds through Christ Jesus.'   (verses 6–7)

'I have learned, in whatever state I am, to be content.'
(verse 11)

'I can do all things through Christ who strengthens me.'
(verse 13)

'My God shall supply all your need according to His riches in glory by Christ Jesus.'   (verse 19)

And in John chapter 20 I read:

'Peace to you! As the Father has sent Me, I also send you,'   (verse 21)

and

> *'Blessed are those who have not seen and yet have believed.'* (verse 29)

All these verses were reassuring but it was the last two that had me convinced. When I told Doug about Joseph's telephone-call I was quick to share with him what I had read but he did not have peace. What if we changed our tickets and then the convention dates were changed back to the original dates? What if the convention was cancelled altogether? The next few days we just prayed and asked the Lord what to do. On 3rd April we read,

> *'Trust in the Lord with all your heart,*
> *And lean not on your own understanding;*
> *In all your ways acknowledge Him,*
> *And He shall direct your paths.'* (Proverbs 3:5–6)

I also asked a good friend, Chris, to pray. She knew we were planning a trip to the Philippines but I did not tell her the dates had been changed. All I said was, 'Please pray for us concerning the trip. Something has cropped up and we're not sure what to do.'

The following morning Chris rang and said she had been praying for us and the Lord had given her a mental picture (vision) of two cog-wheels which were out of alignment, but were coming back into alignment. When Doug and I talked about it we thought that maybe it meant that Joseph would change the dates back again, i.e. bring them back into alignment with us. But then Chris rang again. The Lord had given her another picture, this time of an extending ladder. Immediately we knew we had misinterpreted the previous picture. It was we who were out of alignment and we would have to extend our stay in the Philippines!

(This was really walking by faith for Chris as she had no idea what the situation was and could easily have thought that her two pictures were just her imagination. If she had

156

not mixed them with faith and told us, we would not have known what the Lord wanted to show us!)

Now I wanted to know how we had made the mistake. As I asked Him to show me, Jesus spoke to my heart:

'Your first thought was to have an open ticket. When you heard it would cost extra, your reasoning got in – 21 days would be enough. But I don't want you to have a fixed date. I want you to be led by Me, to live one day at a time, to be free to go where and when I tell you.... Don't limit Me. Leave your affairs so you don't have to rush back to them. If I am to use you, you must be ready whenever I tell you to get up and go....'

As soon as we had asked the Lord to forgive us, we telephoned the travel agent. Changing Doug's ticket from 21 days to an open ticket was quite simple though we had to pay a little extra. My ticket was another matter. Because it was a special package and the ticket had already been issued, there was no way we could change the return date. We had no choice but to forfeit that part of the ticket and buy another for me to return to Hong Kong. Of course, this would cost much more than if I had had an open ticket from the outset. Because we had let our own reasoning affect our decision and had not specifically enquired of the Lord what He wanted, we would have to pay for it. But we also knew that Jesus, in His love and mercy, would provide the extra money we needed. After consulting Him we decided we would wait and get my return ticket in the Philippines when we knew what date we would be leaving there.

Having made this one mistake it was not unnatural to wonder if we had made any other mistakes. I asked the Lord again about the Aglow convention. Now that the other convention dates had been changed, we would have an extra week between the two. As I asked Jesus about it a verse came to my mind:

'Whatsoever is not of faith is sin.'

(Romans 14:23, KJV)

He was obviously taking us into a deeper walk of faith but we knew there was a fine line between faith and presumption. The only way we could avoid presumption was by keeping close to Jesus. At the same time as Jesus had told us how we had made the mistake, He had also said to me:

> 'You must stay in constant communion with Me. How can I *"guide you with My eye"* (Psalm 32:8b) if you are not looking at Me? I want you to be sensitive to My every wish so you can truly say you *"have the mind of Christ"* (1 Corinthians 2:16b).'

17th April came and I flew to Manila with several other ladies. We stayed in a luxurious 5-star hotel about ten minutes' walk from the convention centre. The programme was packed and when Doug arrived on the afternoon of the 20th April I was quite exhausted. We rested a little and then went to the evening meeting which was also the final session. The following day, a Sunday, we were due to leave that hotel but we had no idea what we were going to do. As we now had two-and-a-half weeks before the Baguio convention, we had felt that the Lord had something specific in mind that might open up during the convention, but nothing had.

We were very tired and did not wake up the next morning until about 9.30 am. We both thought how wonderful it would be if we did not have to rush to be out of our room by midday and could stay in that hotel for another night or two to rest and enjoy its facilities. Although it was part of a package deal, it was still quite expensive at about US$130 a night but we felt it would be worth it. We inquired at the reception desk and were told we would have to pay the normal rate, which would cost us more like US$260 each! That was obviously out of the question, but where were we to go? 'Show us, please, Lord Jesus!'

It was now fast approaching 12 noon and we needed to check out. While I quickly packed our bags, praying in tongues all the time, Doug rang a Christian organisation that we had been told had a guest-house. That was soon ruled out – it was a Sunday and their office was closed. Of course there must be hundreds of hotels in Manila but how could we know where we would find a good one at a reasonable price? More to the point, how could we find the place the Lord wanted us to go?

After continuing to pray in tongues for a while I suddenly remembered that Keith, a friend in Hong Kong, had recently been to the Philippines and he had given us some information before we had come. I quickly found the piece of paper on which I had scribbled some notes. And yes, he had told us the name of a hotel in the district of Ermita, from where we could pick up a bus if we wanted to spend a few days at the beach resort of Puerto Galera. That sounded a good possibility and then it would be handy if the Lord did want us to go to Puerto Galera. Doug got the telephone number from the directory enquiries and rang the hotel. We had no idea what kind of place it would be but they had a double room vacant and it would cost us about US$70 a night. That sounded much more reasonable but not **too** cheap, and we had to believe it was where the Lord wanted that night because He hadn't shown us anything else.

We checked out, got a taxi to the hotel and booked in. It would do for a night and then, as no door of ministry had opened up, we could possibly go to Puerto Galera to relax for a few days.

We rested in our room for several hours and then went out to explore. As we walked along Mabini Street we could see there was a big park at the end. It was early Sunday evening and Doug wondered if maybe there would be some kind of open-air evangelistic meeting going on there. We asked the Lord to lead us and as we walked through this large park, which we later found out was Rizal Park, we heard loud voices coming from the midst of a small crowd of people. They were speaking in Tagalog so we could not understand what they were saying but there was obviously a very heated discussion going on.

As we approached the gathering we found two Filipino men shouting angrily at each other. One of them had 'John the Baptist' written on the back of his T-shirt. We asked a by-stander what was going on and he told us they were arguing about religion. One was a Protestant and the other was Roman Catholic. The cheers and boos from the spectators made it obvious that many of them had strong feelings too. Just as the two men in the middle looked like they were about to come to blows, Doug stepped into the 'arena' saying, 'Peace! Peace! Religion is not the answer. Jesus is!'

For the next hour or so he was showing them from the Scriptures how Jesus is the only Man, of all religious leaders, who said,

> *'I am the way, the truth, and the life. No one comes to the Father except through Me.'* (John 14:6)

While Doug was pacifying the two men and eventually got them to shake hands, people standing nearby started asking me questions and I found myself witnessing to several of them. It was an exciting time! When the crowd began drifting away, another young Filipino man came over to Doug and I and asked us many questions. Herman knew his Bible very well and grilled us for quite a while, obviously trying to find out if we were 'kosher' (clean). We must have passed the test because he then asked us how long we would be in Manila as he would like us to take some meetings the following weekend. We explained that we may be going to Puerto Galera the next day but we could telephone him on Friday to see what he had arranged with his elders.

As we walked back through the park to our hotel we were really praising the Lord. We knew He had led us to the right place!

After breakfast the next morning we went to the hotel desk and said we would like to book seats on the bus to Puerto Galera. It was about 10 o'clock and Keith had told us it left every day at 12 o'clock.

'When would you like to go?' the clerk asked us.

'Today, please.'

'I'm very sorry. The bus goes daily at 9 am. But I can book you in for tomorrow.'

Doug and I looked at each other. Obviously the Lord did not want us to go **that** day!

'OK. Thank you. We'll let you know,' we replied and made our way slowly back up to our room. We were on the fourth floor and the lift was out of order.

'Alright, Lord – what do You want us to do? Do You want us to stay here tonight and go to Puerto Galera tomorrow? Or don't You want us to go there at all?'

The more we thought and prayed about it the less comfortable we became about going to Puerto Galera. It would be Tuesday tomorrow and we needed to be back in Manila on Friday to call Herman. But we also did not want to stay in that hotel for so long. According to Keith we should be able to stay in Manila for around 400 pesos a night (approx. US$16 at that time), and even less in Puerto Galera, and we had budgeted accordingly. We wondered if we could find somewhere else in Ermita that was cheaper than where we were, but not too rough. The hotel where we were still seemed expensive for what it was, though we knew it had brought us to the right area of Manila.

While I repacked our bags and prayed, Doug went out to find somewhere else for us to stay. At 11.45 am, 15 minutes before check-out time, he came back with a grin on his face.

'Come on, darling. I've found just the place.'

161

As we checked out and wheeled our bags around the corner, Doug told me he had been to several places but then found this one called the Tropical Mansion. It was a small hotel, obviously a family business, and they had a special offer running in April and May. Apart from 15% off the usual room rate, if we stayed five nights we would get another night free. The room was much nicer than at the previous hotel, and the whole atmosphere of the place was more friendly. We knew this was where the Lord wanted us and we booked in for five nights. When we worked it out over six nights it only cost us US$17 per night! It was much more pleasant and we had peace. Thank You, Jesus!

The rest of the week we stayed in our room in the mornings, resting, reading the Bible, praying and fellowshipping with Jesus. In the afternoons we went out to explore the area and we always found at least one person to talk to about Jesus. We would return to the hotel in the evenings praising the Lord for what He had done.

We met Herman on Saturday and we had a wonderful time of fellowship with him and other brothers and sisters, including speaking at a funeral!

The next morning we were wondering if we should book another six nights in the hotel. We spent the morning seeking the Lord. What did **He** want us to do? Should we go to Puerto Galera this week or should we stay in Manila? Or perhaps there was something else He wanted us to do. As I was asking Jesus this, I felt Him speak to my heart:

'I want you to rest and relax and enjoy Me. I want you to learn to relax wherever you are, whether you are at a beautiful beach resort or in a room in central Manila. It is not dependent on outward circumstances or surroundings, but it comes from within – being still within. The children of Israel could not enter into My rest because of unbelief.'

Once we had made the decision to stay we had peace, and the next few days we continued doing what we had been doing the previous week – spending the mornings in our hotel room, praying, reading the Bible and worshipping Jesus, and going out somewhere to explore in the afternoons.

Two days into that second week we both felt restless because we had not met anybody to talk to about Jesus. The next day we really prayed that the Lord would lead us to the right person or people whose hearts He had prepared. But again we did not meet anybody. We were really dissatisfied.

'Lord! Are we in the right place? Did we make a mistake by staying here this week?'

As we cried out to Jesus to show us what was wrong we both suddenly realised what He was saying. He was showing us that He wants us to get our satisfaction in **Him**, from our relationship with **Him** – not from our ministry or what we do for Him. We felt good and were satisfied when we knew we were being useful, which was fine, but we would be even more useful when we delighted ourselves in Jesus and sought our satisfaction in Him rather than in the ministry. Otherwise we would be dissatisfied if we did not see anything happen, and that is not faith.

> *'Blessed are those who have not seen and yet have believed.'* (John 20:29)

Once again we were aware that the Lord Jesus was drawing us into a new, deeper walk of faith in every area of our lives because it is *'through faith and patience* [we] *inherit the promises'* (Hebrews 6:12).

Joy flooded our hearts. It did not matter if we did not witness to somebody, if the day was not what **we** thought to be profitable spiritually. That was not to be our focus. Our focus was just to enjoy Jesus and worship Him. This is such an important truth. The world is full of Christians

163

who are so busy working for God that they have forgotten Who it is they are working for! Jesus is pushed aside; ministry is the main issue. Does Jesus feel rejected or lonely? He created us to have fellowship with Him (1 Corinthians 1:9) and when Adam and Eve had sinned in the Garden of Eden, He came looking for them (Genesis 3:8). It is that love relationship with Jesus that satisfies His heart and it is only when we satisfy Him that we ourselves will be satisfied. It is also only out of that fellowship with Jesus that we can ever be useful for Him.

> *'I am the vine, you are the branches. He who abides in Me, and I in him, bears much fruit; for without Me you can do nothing.'* (John 15:5)

We had to laugh to ourselves when we realised the Lord Jesus had kept us in Manila for two weeks just to teach us to rest, to enjoy Him, and to be satisfied in Him, no matter where we were or what we were doing. *'His way is perfect'* (Psalm 18:30).

Now it was almost time to meet Pastor Joseph in Baguio.

Chapter 21

The 40th Day

This convention further stretched my faith. Doug had been preaching for years but I hadn't. I had frequently shared in our local fellowship meetings and occasionally spoken more formally at women's meetings and one or two churches we had been invited to, but it was usually Doug who did the speaking. I always felt more comfortable speaking informally to individuals. This was a time, however, when Jesus wanted me to step out of that 'comfort zone', having to rely a hundred per cent on Him.

On 1st May, about a week before the Baguio convention, I was getting very concerned about what I was going to speak on. Jesus, in His love and faithfulness, spoke to me through His Word that day:

> 'I will pour out My Spirit on you;
> I will make My words known to you.'   (Proverbs 1:23)

This was wonderful assurance for me as I mixed those words with faith. I did not even know how many times I would be asked to speak. It was all going to have to be by faith in the Lord's ability, not mine. After all,

> 'I can do all things through Christ who strengthens me.'
> (Philippians 4:13)

We did not see the convention programme until the day before it began and we found we had both been scheduled to speak at one main meeting each of the three days, and also at one workshop each day. Pastor Joseph also asked us if we could fill in at other workshops if the scheduled speakers did not arrive. The end result was that we both spoke at least three times each day!

After the convention finished we were asked to stay a bit longer because several churches in the area wanted us to go and speak at their meetings. Every evening and most afternoons the next week we visited the different churches. We were then asked to go to some other provinces to speak but we felt it was more important to consolidate what we had already started in the convention and to encourage the people to read more, to be able to hear what He was saying to them each day and to develop their love relationship with Jesus. With this in mind, the following week we held a mini Bible-School for all those who wanted to attend. Each morning after all of us read the same four chapters of the Bible, we encouraged everybody to share what the Lord had spoken to them, to train them to be *able ministers of the new testament'* (2 Corinthians 3:6).

Whether it was at the convention, in a church, or in the Bible-School, it was very rare that I knew ahead of time what the Lord Jesus wanted me to talk about. Often I did not know till I got up to speak. But of course, Jesus never failed me. I opened my mouth and He filled it, according to His promise in Psalm 81:10,

'Open your mouth wide, and I will fill it.'

I was thrilled with Jesus' faithfulness.

One day while we were still in Manila, Doug and I had been talking and wondering how long we would stay in the Philippines. Immediately afterwards, we continued reading our Bibles where we had left off a few minutes before. The first verse we read jumped out at us:

'They returned from spying out the land after forty days.'
(Numbers 13:25)

'Forty days! That's a long time. But if that's what You want Lord, then You'll have to confirm it and You'll have to open up the way!'

At this point we had only been there eighteen days. If we stayed for the weekend after the convention, it would still only be twenty-six days. We knew it had to be God if we were to stay another two weeks after that!

On the first day of the mini Bible-School, Tuesday 21st May, one of the chapters we had asked the students to read was Acts 1. When we reached the third verse Doug and I looked at each other. It said

> '. . . being seen by them during **forty** days and speaking of the things pertaining to the Kingdom of God.'

It was hard for us not to laugh out loud! I quickly calculated when we would have been in the Philippines forty days. I had arrived in Manila three days before Doug and my fortieth day would be the following Monday, the 27th May. With two verses saying forty days we knew that was the day we must leave. As we also had meetings in the afternoon on that Tuesday and Wednesday, it was Thursday before we could go to the travel agent. The following is part of the newsletter we sent out after we returned to Hong Kong:

We went to the travel agent to book our return flights for Monday 27th May – exactly forty days since Helen had arrived. We had been teaching a lot about living by faith in every area of our lives and the Lord was testing us right to the end. But like we have often said, it is not **our faith** that is important, but God's **faithfulness**!

Also, while in Manila we had been to a Cathay Pacific office to inquire about the price of a one-way ticket to Hong Kong for Helen. They had just received notice of a special offer: instead of US$194 (Economy class), she could go on the evening flight for US$110 (Hotel class). The travel agent in Baguio had not heard about this special offer, but after we insisted, he rang the Manila office to find it was true. After we'd booked and paid for my Hotel-class ticket (Doug's ticket was already paid for), the travel agent suddenly said there was only one problem – no seat available in Hotel class! He had booked Doug's seat in Economy class and wait-listed Helen in Hotel class! This was Thursday afternoon; we could collect our tickets on Saturday afternoon. We booked seats on the bus for Monday morning to make the 8-hour journey to Manila.

When Doug went to collect the tickets he returned with only his. There was still no seat for Helen, and we would have to pick up her ticket on Monday from the travel agent's main office when we arrived in Manila. Time-wise, that was cutting it very fine. The bus might not arrive in Manila till 4.30 pm, depending on traffic, and we were supposed to be at the airport by 5 pm. We had heard about the notorious traffic jams in downtown Manila and now we also had to travel across the city to the travel agent. How long it would take was dependent on that traffic – and, of course, the Lord! After a few moments of inner panic Helen came back into a rest. After all, it was the Lord who had said we were to leave after forty days so it was His responsibility to get her on the plane! Thank You, Jesus! Occasionally during the next few hours the thought, 'What if . . . ?' kept coming back, but we knew it was a test. We had to mix what the Lord had told us with faith – and, by God's grace, we were able to hold fast *'the confession of our faith without wavering; (for He is faithful that promised)'* (Hebrews 10:23, KJV).

The bus arrived in Manila at 3.30 pm. We had an hour extra. Hallelujah! We first went to the Cathay Pacific office to check if there was a seat available. Yes, there was – but the travel agent had not confirmed the booking and it was too late to put her on the passenger list even for Economy class! We refused the offer of a seat on the following day – 'Lord! **You** said **forty** days!' We knew it would have to be a miracle to get Helen on that plane but we have a miracle-working God.

We then went to the travel agent, presented Helen's receipt, and said we had come for the ticket which we had booked and paid for in Baguio, making no mention that there may be a problem. We sat there praying in tongues quietly, while two girls tapped away at their computers, conferred together and made several phone-calls. This went on for over half an hour! It was obvious there was some complication! But as long as we kept our eyes on Jesus, peace ruled in our hearts. Eventually one of the girls wrote out a ticket, handed it to us and wished us a good flight! There was no mention of any difficulty! We left the travel agency rejoicing!

Now we had to get to the airport. It was 4.40 pm, the beginning of rush hour. The taxi soon got stuck in the traffic. Our driver was not happy and said we would have to get out and get another taxi. We calmly told him we could not get another taxi there in the middle of the traffic(!) so he continued driving and we continued praying in tongues. Then, before we knew it, he turned off into a side street, by-passed the congested area and we arrived at the airport at exactly 5 pm! We had never been at an airport so promptly before! Wonderful, wonderful Jesus! He is faithful to the end!

Chapter 22

Faith or Presumption

There is a fine line between faith and presumption. If God tells us to do something then we should do it – in faith. And when He does tell us, He gives us the faith to go with it because

> *'Faith comes by hearing, and hearing by the word of God.'* (Romans 10:17)

However, if we do something that the Lord has not told us to do, He is not committed to His promises. For example, if we **accidentally** drink some poison God's promise is that it will not harm us:

> *'These signs will follow those who believe ... if they drink anything deadly, it will by no means hurt them.'*
> (Mark 16:17–18)

The important word here is 'if'- it does not say 'when'.

When Jesus was in the wilderness for forty days before He began His ministry, the devil came to Him and said,

> *' "If you are the Son of God, throw Yourself down. For it is written: 'He shall give His angels charge over you,' and 'In their hands they shall bear you up, lest you dash your foot against a stone.' "*
>
> *Jesus said to him, "It is written again, 'You shall not tempt the Lord your God.' " '*   (Matthew 4:6–7)

The devil quoted the Bible promises so why did Jesus say that was tempting God? The reason is that the devil missed a very important line out of the promise: *' ...to keep you in all your ways...'* (Psalm 91:11–12), which means 'in all your **ordinary** ways'. If we deliberately do something dangerous we cannot expect the Lord to help us or to keep us safe unless He Himself has told us to do it. It is presumption.

One time when Doug and I first came to Hong Kong we went into China for a month, travelling around to see whether the Lord had something for us to do there. Before we started off on the trip we asked the Lord Jesus to lead us and guide us and He opened up a way for us to go to Beijing for two weeks, all expenses paid, looking after two little girls while their parents were away. We knew for sure that that was right because before we came to Hong Kong somebody in Israel had asked us to give a letter to a friend of theirs in China if we should ever meet him in all the 1.2 billion people there. At the time we thought that extremely unlikely! But when we were asked if we would look after these two children, and we had felt it was right to do so, we found out it was the same man for whom we had the letter!

When the girls' father returned we left Beijing and felt to go to Shanghai for a few days and then on to Hangzhou and Changsha. These were all open cities because at that time (1984) there were twenty-nine cities throughout China which were designated as being open to foreign tourists. These were the only places we were officially allowed to visit. Enjoying adventure, we thought it would be interesting to visit somewhere other than these cities. Before leaving Changsha we decided not to ride the train all the way to Guangzhou just yet, but get off at a place called Zhuzhou, about two hours south of Changsha. In our travel book it said there was a hotel there and it gave directions how to get to it from the railway station. We followed the directions and soon found ourselves at the hotel – a rather drab, grey building. As we approached the desk one of the receptionists saw us and started pointing to us, saying something very emphatically and shaking her head. Of course we didn't understand the words she was speaking but we could easily understand from her actions that she was not too happy to see us and did not want us to stay!

'Oh, dear! What are we going to do now?' I thought. 'Lord! Have we made a mistake coming here? Forgive us, Lord, **please**! And **help** us!'

We remained standing with our bags as the receptionists huddled together, talking amongst themselves, pointing and nodding towards us.

'We better do some praying,' Doug whispered to me, and under our breath we started praying. We soon ran out of English and continued in tongues.

After several l-o-n-g minutes one young lady detached herself from the rest of the group and came towards us. Taking hold of our luggage trolley and beckoning to us, we knew she wanted us to follow her. Out of the hotel, along the main street, down a side street and into another large building, we followed her, all the time praying quietly in tongues. I had a horrible feeling that we had acted presumptuously in coming to this 'closed city' and repeatedly asked the Lord to forgive us if we had, to have mercy on us and help us anyway. In this second building there was a brief exchange between the receptionist and an older woman behind the desk who, from the shaking of her head and wave of her hand, made it very clear that we could not stay there either. Meekly we turned round and followed the receptionist out into the street. She was still pulling our luggage trolley and setting quite a pace as we tried to keep up with her through the crowds. It was raining lightly and beginning to get dark as we entered through an archway into the courtyard of a very formidable looking building.

'Dear me! This looks like a police station or a prison,' I whispered to Doug. I was beginning to get a little frightened. 'Lord – please have mercy on us and forgive us. **Please** find us a place to stay.'

As we went into the building we could see it was neither. Heaving a sigh of relief for that but still desperately praying in tongues, we waited as 'our' receptionist talked with the receptionist there. Then an older man was called in and the debate continued for several more minutes. I began to feel a little more hopeful as the head-shakings subsided and were replaced with faint nods.

'Lord – please give us favour. Thank You, Jesus. Nothing's too difficult for You.'

After what seemed an age, the older man turned to us and in halting English asked us how long we wanted to stay.

'Only one night. One night will be OK please.'

'One night. Yes, one night,' he hurriedly agreed. 'No stay more. One night, then you go. Tomorrow, 12 o'clock, you go.'

We readily assented and thanked our receptionist profusely as she let go of our luggage trolley, turned and left the hotel. Thanking the man for his help, we followed him as he showed us to our room and told us what time dinner would be served. When he left I sighed with relief, 'Oh, thank You, **thank** You, Jesus!'

The next morning we asked the receptionist where we could buy train tickets to Guangzhou. She called the older man from the previous night who told us we had to go to the railway station. In all the other places we had been, foreigners were not allowed to buy tickets at the railway station but only at special 'China Travel' agencies within the hotels. As this was not an open city and tourists were not expected to be there, there was obviously no China Travel Service.

In the railway station we queued up for over half an hour at the ticket desk. When we got to the counter I pointed in our travel book to the number of the train to Guangzhou and lifted two fingers signifying we wanted two tickets. At the same time I pushed the approximate amount of money towards the clerk. Pushing the money back to me she waved two tickets.

'Yes,' I said, nodding vigorously and pushing the

money back to her. 'Two tickets for tonight's train to Guangzhou.'

The clerk also nodded, pushed the money back to me and again waved the tickets at me.

Puzzled, I looked at Doug. 'Try again,' he urged.

Again I pointed in the book to the exact train, date and type of ticket. Again she waved the tickets at me, pleasantly but firmly, saying something in Mandarin.

We couldn't understand what she was trying to tell us and the people in line behind us were getting a little upset that we were taking so long, so we stepped aside to let the next person buy their ticket.

'Lord Jesus – what should we do? Please help us to get the train tickets.'

We looked around the station for somebody who might speak English and could tell us what to do. We approached several people but no, they did not speak English. When we pointed in our travel book to try to explain what we wanted, each of them pointed to another section of the station. Following the direction they pointed to, we found ourselves in a huge, almost deserted lobby area. Looking around we could not see any ticket office or any officials. I again asked Jesus to forgive us for getting ourselves into this situation and asked Him to please help us to leave Zhuzhou. Continuing to pray in tongues, we stood there waiting for the Lord to show us what to do.

Suddenly seeing a man in uniform entering the area, we went over to him. As I pointed in our travel book again he nodded and beckoned us to follow him. He took us through a door at the far end of the lobby area, up some steps, along a corridor and into an office. Explaining something to a lady at a desk, he left us there. She looked at where we pointed in our travel guide and started to write in a small book. Then, tearing the piece of paper out of the book, she handed it to another young man and signalled us to follow him. He led us back along the corridor, down the stairs, across the huge lobby area, through to the ticket office area of the station, past the long line of people queuing and right up to the ticket counter we had just left. Handing the desk clerk the piece of paper, he left us. Smiling broadly, the lady nodded emphatically, took our money from us and gave us our tickets! Thanking her profusely we fairly danced out of that railway station. 'Thank You, thank You, Jesus! Praise You, Lord Jesus!'

Our curiosity and desire for adventure had brought us a little more 'adventure' than we had bargained for! Looking back I can see that we had acted **presumptuously** in getting off the train in Zhuzhou. We had done something the Lord had not told us to do and we had to ask Him to forgive us for our presumption – that is, presuming He would help us in a city where we were not supposed to be! It is possible that the Lord would tell us to go somewhere like that, if there was somebody there He wanted us to talk to about Himself or to help in some way. But as it was, we did not talk to anybody about Jesus and only caused a lot of trouble for that poor receptionist in the first hotel we went to. Bless her in the Name of Jesus for all her help! As much as she did it for us, she did it for Jesus (Matthew 25:40), although she does not know it.

I thank Jesus that although we had done something presumptuously, He forgave us because

'If we confess our sins, He is faithful and just to forgive us our sins and to cleanse us from all unrighteousness.'
(1 John 1:9)

In His love and mercy He still helped us to find a place to stay and to get our tickets out of there. We had made a mistake, but we had also learnt a lesson! Perhaps, if we had not asked Jesus to forgive us and had stubbornly insisted that He had led us to Zhuzhou, things may not have ended up so well!

This made me even more determined to do only what Jesus wanted and not what I wanted. I did not even want to do the good thing if it was not God because sometimes the 'good' can be the enemy of the 'best'. When Adam and Eve were in the garden of Eden there were many trees there:

> 'The tree of life was also in the midst of the garden, and the tree of the knowledge of good and evil. . . . And the Lord God commanded the man, saying, "Of every tree of the garden you may freely eat; but of the tree of the knowledge of good and evil you shall not eat, for in the day that you eat of it you shall surely die." '
>
> (Genesis 2:9, 16–17)

Most of us would not want to do something that was evil, but it is interesting that the good is from the same tree as the evil! When we do what Jesus tells us to do it will not only be good, it will be **life**!

A Final Word

'Therefore, there is now no condemnation for those who are in Christ Jesus [who do not live according to their sinful nature but **according to the Spirit**] *because through Christ Jesus the law of the Spirit of life set me free from the law of sin and death. For what the law was powerless to do in that it was weakened by our sinful nature, **God did** by sending His own Son in the likeness of sinful man to be a sin offering. And so he condemned sin in sinful man, in order that the righteous requirements of the law might be fully met in us, who do not live according to our sinful nature but **according to the Spirit**.*

*Those who live according to their sinful nature have their minds set on what that nature desires; but those who live in accordance with the Spirit have their minds set on what the Spirit desires. The mind of sinful man is death, but **the mind controlled by the Spirit is life and peace**, because the sinful mind is hostile to God. It does not submit to God's law, nor can it do so. Those controlled by their sinful nature cannot please God.*

You, however, are controlled not by your sinful nature but by the Spirit, if the Spirit of God lives in you. And if anyone does not have the Spirit of Christ, he does not belong to Christ. But if Christ is in you, your body is dead because of sin, yet your spirit is alive because of righteousness. And if the Spirit of him who raised Jesus from the dead is living in you, he who raised Christ from the dead will also give life to your mortal bodies through his Spirit, who lives in you.

*. . . those who are **led by the Spirit of God** are sons of God. . . . Now if we are children, then we are heirs – heirs of God and co-heirs with Christ, if indeed **we share in***

his sufferings in order that we may also share in his glory.'
(Romans 8:1–17, NIV)

It is not you and I that can live the life that Jesus wants us to live. It is the Spirit of God, the Holy Spirit, who is the life of Jesus living within us. As we allow Him to live in us and through us, He will give us the ability, the grace, the strength and the wisdom to do whatever He wants; that which is pleasing to Him and that which satisfies Him. My own efforts will never get me anywhere except in a legal bondage of dos and don'ts.

'Abide in Me, and I in you. As the branch cannot bear fruit of itself, unless it abides in the vine, neither can you unless you abide in Me. I am the vine, you are the branches. He who abides in Me, and I in him, bears much fruit; for without Me you can do nothing.'
(John 15:4–5)

But

'I can do all things through Christ who strengthens me.'
(Philippians 4:13)

Why have I quoted all the above scriptures?

Because I am aware that some people reading this book may feel condemned because they are not doing some of the things I have suggested, and perhaps others will try to do them in their own strength. The purpose of this book is certainly not to make anybody feel condemned. And we can never do the things I have mentioned by ourselves. It is Jesus in us, and can only be Jesus in us, who can first of all give us the desire to live a life well-pleasing to Him, and then actually live His life through us. All He wants is for us to ask Him to help us and then allow Him to do it.

The only reason why I have written all the things in this book is so that you and I will be ready to go through the Tribulation if we need to, and be ready to meet Jesus, either when we die or when He comes for His bride. If you do want to be ready, then you can very simply pray the following prayer, from your heart:

'Lord Jesus – I confess that I have done wrong things but I thank You that You took the punishment for those sins when You died on the Cross. I ask you now to forgive me for all my sins and to cleanse me by Your Blood. I also choose to forgive all those who have hurt me in the past [name those people specifically] as You have forgiven me, and I ask You to bless those people so that they too may come to know You. I want to have a meaningful and intimate relationship with You. Even though You are the Creator of the Universe, I want to be Your friend. I also want You to be the Lord of my life and I know I cannot live a life well-pleasing to You by myself so I ask You to come into my heart, live Your life in me, and take control of my life. Thank You. I also ask You to come and fill me with Your Holy Spirit and give me the gift of tongues so I can praise and worship You. Thank You Jesus.

And Lord Jesus, I don't know what the future holds but You do. Please prepare me for the future and give me a hunger to know You better. Help me to organize my time so I can spend time worshipping You, praying and reading the Bible so that I will be ready to meet You when that time comes. Please lead me to a good church or fellowship where I can meet other people who love You and where I can learn and grow spiritually. Lead me by Your Holy Spirit so I can do your will. Help me to live by faith in You because I know You are the faithful One and You will never ask me to do anything without giving me all that's necessary to fulfil Your will. I humbly acknowledge that I need You in every area of my life. I cannot do anything without You but I know I can do all things through You who strengthens me.

Lord Jesus – please give me a revelation of Yourself and Your love for me. I love You, Lord Jesus, but I want to love You more. Help me to fall in love with You each day. I thank You and praise You, Lord Jesus, for hearing and answering my prayer and I give You all the glory for what You are going to do in and through me. I pray in Your Name, Lord Jesus Christ of Nazareth, Amen!'

Appendix

Daily Bible Reading Chart

There are many different ways of reading through the Bible. To help you, I would like to suggest two alternative ways of reading. One is to try to read a whole book of the Bible each day. Of course, that is much easier with the shorter books, like the New Testament Epistles, and the Old Testament minor prophets. The longer books can be read over several days. Most people, with most ordinary books, start reading a book at the beginning and continue until the end. Why should the Bible be any different?

But because some parts of it, especially in the Old Testament, are not as interesting as others, I would recommend another way of reading, something like the following Bible Reading plan that was worked out by the nineteenth century Scottish minister, Dr Robert Murray McCheyne. If used systematically the whole Bible can be read over a period of one, two or four years (though I recommend that you try doing it in one year and then repeat it every year). This plan provides a balanced daily diet of both Old and New Testaments, and is increasingly used by church fellowships to harmonise and bring into unity, the systematic personal Bible reading of their members.

Know Your Bible has been published by Mill Grove, 10 Crescent Road, South Woodford, London E18 1JB. Mill Grove is a children's home, run as a large 'family' which cares for children in need and was started in 1899 by Herbert White. Since then three principles have undergirded their life:

- caring for children whose families are in difficulty,
- sharing with them the love of Jesus Christ, and
- asking God alone to meet the needs of the family.

Throughout the twentieth century God has answered their prayers and honoured the trust placed in Him. May He also honour the trust **you** place in Him. Amen!

January

This is my beloved Son, with whom I am well pleased; listen to him

MORNING			Day	EVENING		
Gen.	1	Matt.	1 – 1 –	Ezra	1	Acts	1
"	2	"	2 – 2 –	"	2	"	2
"	3	"	3 – 3 –	"	3	"	3
"	4	"	4 – 4 –	"	4	"	4
"	5	"	5 – 5 –	"	5	"	5
"	6	"	6 – 6 –	"	6	"	6
"	7	"	7 – 7 –	"	7	"	7
"	8	"	8 – 8 –	"	8	"	8
"	9–10	"	9 – 9 –	"	9	"	9
"	11	"	10 – 10 –	"	10	"	10
"	12	"	11 – 11 –	Neh.	1	"	11
"	13	"	12 – 12 –	"	2	"	12
"	14	"	13 – 13 –	"	3	"	13
"	15	"	14 – 14 –	"	4	"	14
"	16	"	15 – 15 –	"	5	"	15
"	17	"	16 – 16 –	"	6	"	16
"	18	"	17 – 17 –	"	7	"	17
"	19	"	18 – 18 –	"	8	"	18
"	20	"	19 – 19 –	"	9	"	19
"	21	"	20 – 20 –	"	10	"	20
"	22	"	21 – 21 –	"	11	"	21
"	23	"	22 – 22 –	"	12	"	22
"	24	"	23 – 23 –	"	13	"	23
"	25	"	24 – 24 –	Esther	1	"	24
"	26	"	25 – 25 –	"	2	"	25
"	27	"	26 – 26 –	"	3	"	26
"	28	"	27 – 27 –	"	4	"	27
"	29	"	28 – 28 –	"	5	"	28
"	30	Mark	1 – 29 –	"	6	Rom.	1
"	31	"	2 – 30 –	"	7	"	2
"	32	"	3 – 31 –	"	8	"	3

February

I have esteemed the words of his mouth more than my necessary food

	MORNING			Day		EVENING		
Gen.	33	Mark	4	– 1 –	Esther	9–10	Rom.	4
"	34	"	5	– 2 –	Job	1	"	5
"	35–36	"	6	– 3 –	"	2	"	6
"	37	"	7	– 4 –	"	3	"	7
"	38	"	8	– 5 –	"	4	"	8
"	39	"	9	– 6 –	"	5	"	9
"	40	"	10	– 7 –	"	6	"	10
"	41	"	11	– 8 –	"	7	"	11
"	42	"	12	– 9 –	"	8	"	12
"	43	"	13	– 10 –	"	9	"	13
"	44	"	14	– 11 –	"	10	"	14
"	45	"	15	– 12 –	"	11	"	15
"	46	"	16	– 13 –	"	12	"	16
"	47	Luke	1:1–38	– 14 –	"	13	1 Cor.	1
"	48	"	1:39–80	– 15 –	"	14	"	2
"	49	"	2	– 16 –	"	15	"	3
"	50	"	3	– 17 –	"	16–17	"	4
Exodus	1	"	4	– 18 –	"	18	"	5
"	2	"	5	– 19 –	"	19	"	6
"	3	"	6	– 20 –	"	20	"	7
"	4	"	7	– 21 –	"	21	"	8
"	5	"	8	– 22 –	"	22	"	9
"	6	"	9	– 23 –	"	23	"	10
"	7	"	10	– 24 –	"	24	"	11
"	8	"	11	– 25 –	"	25–26	"	12
"	9	"	12	– 26 –	"	27	"	13
"	10	"	13	– 27 –	"	28	"	14
"	11–12:20	"	14	– 28 –	"	29	"	15

March

Mary kept all these things, pondering them in her heart

	MORNING			Day		EVENING		
Ex.	12:21–51	Luke	15	– 1 –	Job	30	1 Cor	16
"	13	"	16	– 2 –	"	31	2 Cor.	1
"	14	"	17	– 3 –	"	32	"	2
"	15	"	18	– 4 –	"	33	"	3
"	16	"	19	– 5 –	"	34	"	4
"	17	"	20	– 6 –	"	35	"	5
"	18	"	21	– 7 –	"	36	"	6

MORNING				Day	EVENING			
Exodus	19	Luke	22	– 8 –	Job	37	2 Cor.	7
"	20	"	23	– 9 –	"	38	"	8
"	21	"	24	– 10 –	"	39	"	9
"	22	John	1	– 11 –	"	40	"	10
"	23	"	2	– 12 –	"	41	"	11
"	24	"	3	– 13 –	"	42	"	12
"	25	"	4	– 14 –	Prov.	1	"	13
"	26	"	5	– 15 –	"	2	Gal.	1
"	27	"	6	– 16 –	"	3	"	2
"	28	"	7	– 17 –	"	4	"	3
"	29	"	8	– 18 –	"	5	"	4
"	30	"	9	– 19 –	"	6	"	5
"	31	"	10	– 20 –	"	7	"	6
"	32	"	11	– 21 –	"	8	Eph.	1
"	33	"	12	– 22 –	"	9	"	2
"	34	"	13	– 23 –	"	10	"	3
"	35	"	14	– 24 –	"	11	"	4
"	36	"	15	– 25 –	"	12	"	5
"	37	"	16	– 26 –	"	13	"	6
"	38	"	17	– 27 –	"	14	Phil.	1
"	39	"	18	– 28 –	"	15	"	2
"	40	"	19	– 29 –	"	16	"	3
Lev.	1	"	20	– 30 –	"	17	"	4
"	2–3	"	21	– 31 –	"	18	Col.	1

April

O send out thy light and thy truth;
let them lead me

MORNING				Day	EVENING			
Lev.	4	Psalms	1–2	– 1 –	Prov.	19	Col.	2
"	5	"	3–4	– 2 –	"	20	"	3
"	6	"	5–6	– 3 –	"	21	"	4
"	7	"	7–8	– 4 –	"	22	1 Thes.	1
"	8	"	9	– 5 –	"	23	"	2
"	9	"	10	– 6 –	"	24	"	3
"	10	"	11–12	– 7 –	"	25	"	4
"	11–12	"	13–14	– 8 –	"	26	"	5
"	13	"	15–16	– 9 –	"	27	2 Thes.	1
"	14	"	17	– 10 –	"	28	"	2
"	15	"	18	– 11 –	"	29	"	3
"	16	"	19	– 12 –	"	30	1 Tim.	1
"	17	"	20–21	– 13 –	"	31	"	2
"	18	"	22	– 14 –	Eccles.	1	"	3

	MORNING		Day		EVENING	
Lev.	19	Psalms 23–24	– 15 –	Eccles.	2	1 Tim.	4
"	20	" 25	– 16 –	"	3	"	5
"	21	" 26–27	– 17 –	"	4	"	6
"	22	" 28–29	– 18 –	"	5	2 Tim.	1
"	23	" 30	– 19 –	"	6	"	2
"	24	" 31	– 20 –	"	7	"	3
"	25	" 32	– 21 –	"	8	"	4
"	26	" 33	– 22 –	"	9	Titus	1
"	27	" 34	– 23 –	"	10	"	2
Num.	1	" 35	– 24 –	"	11	"	3
"	2	" 36	– 25 –	"	12	Philm.	1
"	3	" 37	– 26 –	Song	1	Heb.	1
"	4	" 38	– 27 –	"	2	"	2
"	5	" 39	– 28 –	"	3	"	3
"	6	" 40–41	– 29 –	"	4	"	4
"	7	" 42–43	– 30 –	"	5	"	5

May

*From a child thou hast known
the holy scriptures*

	MORNING		Day		EVENING	
Num.	8	Psalms 44	– 1 –	Song	6	Heb.	6
"	9	" 45	– 2 –	"	7	"	7
"	10	" 46–47	– 3 –	"	8	"	8
"	11	" 48	– 4 –	Isaiah	1	"	9
"	12–13	" 49	– 5 –	"	2	"	10
"	14	" 50	– 6 –	"	3–4	"	11
"	15	" 51	– 7 –	"	5	"	12
"	16	" 52–54	– 8 –	"	6	"	13
"	17–18	" 55	– 9 –	"	7	James	1
"	19	" 56–57	– 10 –	"	8–9:7	"	2
"	20	" 58–59	– 11 –	"	9:8–10:4	"	3
"	21	" 60–61	– 12 –	"	10:5–34	"	4
"	22	" 62–63	– 13 –	"	11–12	"	5
"	23	" 64–65	– 14 –	"	13	1 Peter	1
"	24	" 66–67	– 15 –	"	14	"	2
"	25	" 68	– 16 –	"	15	"	3
"	26	" 69	– 17 –	"	16	"	4
"	27	" 70–71	– 18 –	"	17–18	"	5
"	28	" 72	– 19 –	"	19–20	2 Peter	1
"	29	" 73	– 20 –	"	21	"	2
"	30	" 74	– 21 –	"	22	"	3
"	31	" 75–76	– 22 –	"	23	1 John	1

June

Blessed is he that readeth and they that hear

July

MORNING				Day		EVENING			
Joshua	3	Ps.	126–128	– 1 –	Isaiah		63	Matt.	11
"	4	"	129–131	– 2 –	"		64	"	12
"	5–6:5	"	132–134	– 3 –	"		65	"	13
"	6:6–27	"	135–136	– 4 –	"		66	"	14
"	7	"	137–138	– 5 –	Jer.		1	"	15
"	8	"	139	– 6 –	"		2	"	16
"	9	"	140–141	– 7 –	"		3	"	17
"	10	"	142–143	– 8 –	"		4	"	18
"	11	"	144	– 9 –	"		5	"	19
"	12–13	"	145	– 10 –	"		6	"	20
"	14–15	"	146–147	– 11 –	"		7	"	21
"	16–17	"	148	– 12 –	"		8	"	22
"	18–19	"	149–150	– 13 –	"		9	"	23
"	20–21	Acts	1	– 14 –	"		10	"	24
"	22	"	2	– 15 –	"		11	"	25
"	23	"	3	– 16 –	"		12	"	26
"	24	"	4	– 17 –	"		13	"	27
Judges	1	"	5	– 18 –	"		14	"	28
"	2	"	6	– 19 –	"		15	Mark	1
"	3	"	7	– 20 –	"		16	"	2
"	4	"	8	– 21 –	"		17	"	3
"	5	"	9	– 22 –	"		18	"	4
"	6	"	10	– 23 –	"		19	"	5
"	7	"	11	– 24 –	"		20	"	6
"	8	"	12	– 25 –	"		21	"	7
"	9	"	13	– 26 –	"		22	"	8
"	10–11:11	"	14	– 27 –	"		23	"	9
"	11:12–40	"	15	– 28 –	"		24	"	10
"	12	"	16	– 29 –	"		25	"	11
"	13	"	17	– 30 –	"		26	"	12
"	14	"	18	– 31 –	"		27	"	13

August

MORNING				Day		EVENING			
Judges	15	Acts	19	– 1 –	Jer.		28	Mark	14
"	16	"	20	– 2 –	"		29	"	15
"	17	"	21	– 3 –	"		30–31	"	16
"	18	"	22	– 4 –	"		32	Psalms	1–2

	MORNING			Day	EVENING			
Judges	19	Acts	23	– 5 –	Jer.	33	Psalms	3–4
"	20	"	24	– 6 –	"	34	"	5–6
"	21	"	25	– 7 –	"	35	"	7–8
Ruth	1	"	26	– 8 –	"	36 & 45	"	9
"	2	"	27	– 9 –	"	37	"	10
"	3–4	"	28	– 10 –	"	38	"	11–12
1 Sam.	1	Rom.	1	– 11 –	"	39	"	13–14
"	2	"	2	– 12 –	"	40	"	15–16
"	3	"	3	– 13 –	"	41	"	17
"	4	"	4	– 14 –	"	42	"	18
"	5–6	"	5	– 15 –	"	43	"	19
"	7–8	"	6	– 16 –	"	44	"	20–21
"	9	"	7	– 17 –	"	46	"	22
"	10	"	8	– 18 –	"	47	"	23–24
"	11	"	9	– 19 –	"	48	"	25
"	12	"	10	– 20 –	"	49	"	26–27
"	13	"	11	– 21 –	"	50	"	28–29
"	14	"	12	– 22 –	"	51	"	30
"	15	"	13	– 23 –	"	52	"	31
"	16	"	14	– 24 –	Lam.	1	"	32
"	17	"	15	– 25 –	"	2	"	33
"	18	"	16	– 26 –	"	3	"	34
"	19	1 Cor.	1	– 27 –	"	4	"	35
"	20	"	2	– 28 –	"	5	"	36
"	21–22	"	3	– 29 –	Ezekiel	1	"	37
"	23	"	4	– 30 –	"	2	"	38
"	24	"	5	– 31 –	"	3	"	39

September

*The law of the Lord is perfect,
converting the soul*

	MORNING			Day	EVENING			
1 Sam	25	1 Cor.	6	– 1 –	Ezekiel	4	Psalms	40–41
"	26	"	7	– 2 –	"	5	"	42–43
"	27	"	8	– 3 –	"	6	"	44
"	28	"	9	– 4 –	"	7	"	45
"	29–30	"	10	– 5 –	"	8	"	46–47
"	31	"	11	– 6 –	"	9	"	48
2 Sam.	1	"	12	– 7 –	"	10	"	49
"	2	"	13	– 8 –	"	11	"	50
"	3	"	14	– 9 –	"	12	"	51
"	4–5	"	15	– 10 –	"	13	"	52–54
"	6	"	16	– 11 –	"	14	"	55

MORNING			Day		EVENING		
2 Sam.	7	2 Cor.	1	– 12 –	Exekiel	15	Psalms 56–57
"	8–9	"	2	– 13 –	"	16	" 58–59
"	10	"	3	– 14 –	"	17	" 60–61
"	11	"	4	– 15 –	"	18	" 62–63
"	12	"	5	– 16 –	"	19	" 64–65
"	13	"	6	– 17 –	"	20	" 66–67
"	14	"	7	– 18 –	"	21	" 68
"	15	"	8	– 19 –	"	22	" 69
"	16	"	9	– 20 –	"	23	" 70–71
"	17	"	10	– 21 –	"	24	" 72
"	18	"	11	– 22 –	"	25	" 73
"	19	"	12	– 23 –	"	26	" 74
"	20	"	13	– 24 –	"	27	" 75–76
"	21	Gal.	1	25 –	"	28	" 77
"	22	"	2	– 26 –	"	29	" 78:1–37
"	23	"	3	– 27 –	"	30	" 78:38–72
"	24	"	4	– 28 –	"	31	" 79
1 Kings	1	"	5	– 29 –	"	32	" 80
"	2	"	6	– 30 –	"	33	" 81–82

October

O how I love thy Law!
it is my meditation all the day

MORNING			Day		EVENING		
1 Kings	3	Eph.	1	– 1 –	Ezekiel	34	Psalms 83–84
"	4–5	"	2	– 2 –	"	35	" 85
"	6	"	3	– 3 –	"	36	" 86
"	7	"	4	– 4 –	"	37	" 87–88
"	8	"	5	– 5 –	"	38	" 89
"	9	"	6	– 6 –	"	39	" 90
"	10	Phil.	1	– 7 –	"	40	" 91
"	11	"	2	– 8 –	"	41	" 92–93
"	12	"	3	– 9 –	"	42	" 94
"	13	"	4	– 10 –	"	43	" 95–96
"	14	Col.	1	– 11 –	"	44	" 97–98
"	15	"	2	– 12 –	"	45	" 99–101
"	16	"	3	– 13 –	"	46	" 102
"	17	"	4	– 14 –	"	47	" 103
"	18	1 Thes.	1	– 15 –	"	48	" 104
"	19	"	2	– 16 –	Daniel	1	" 105
"	20	"	3	– 17 –	"	2	" 106
"	21	"	4	– 18 –	"	3	" 107
"	22	"	5	– 19 –	"	4	" 108–109

MORNING				Day	EVENING		
2 Kings	1	2 Thes.	1	– 20 –	Daniel	5	Ps. 110–111
"	2	"	2	– 21 –	"	6	" 112–113
"	3	"	3	– 22 –	"	7	" 114–115
"	4	1 Tim.	1	– 23 –	"	8	" 116
"	5	"	2	– 24 –	"	9	" 117–118
"	6	"	3	– 25 –	"	10	" 119:1–24
"	7	"	4	– 26 –	"	11	"119:25–48
"	8	"	5	– 27 –	"	12	"119:49–72
"	9	"	6	– 28 –	Hosea	1	"119:73–96
"	10	2 Tim.	1	– 29 –	"	2	119:97–120
"	11–12	"	2	– 30 –	"	3–4	119:121–144
"	13	"	3	– 31 –	"	5–6	119:145–176

November

As new-born babes desire the sincere milk of the word that ye may grow thereby

MORNING				Day	EVENING		
2 Kings	14	2 Tim.	4	– 1 –	Hosea	7	Ps. 120–122
"	15	Titus	1	– 2 –	"	8	" 123–125
"	16	"	2	– 3 –	"	9	" 126–128
"	17	"	3	– 4 –	"	10	" 129–131
"	18	Philm.	1	– 5 –	"	11	" 132–134
"	19	Heb.	1	– 6 –	"	12	" 135–136
"	20	"	2	– 7 –	"	13	" 137–138
"	21	"	3	– 8 –	"	14	" 139
"	22	"	4	– 9 –	Joel	1	" 140–141
"	23	"	5	– 10 –	"	2	" 142
"	24	"	6	– 11 –	"	3	" 143
"	25	"	7	– 12 –	Amos	1	" 144
1 Chr.	1–2	"	8	– 13 –	"	2	" 145
"	3–4	"	9	– 14 –	"	3	" 146–147
"	5–6	"	10	– 15 –	"	4	" 148–150
"	7–8	"	11	– 16 –	"	5	Luke 1:1–38
"	9–10	"	12	– 17 –	"	6	" 1:39–80
"	11–12	"	13	– 18 –	"	7	" 2
"	13–14	James	1	– 19 –	"	8	" 3
"	15	"	2	– 20 –	"	9	" 4
"	16	"	3	– 21 –	Obad.	1	" 5
"	17	"	4	– 22 –	Jonah	1	" 6
"	18	"	5	– 23 –	"	2	" 7
"	19–20	1 Peter	1	– 24 –	"	3	" 8
"	21	"	2	– 25 –	"	4	" 9
"	22	"	3	– 26 –	Micah	1	" 10

MORNING			Day	EVENING		
1 Chr.	23	1 Peter	4	– 27 –	Micah	2	Luke	11
"	24–25	"	5	– 28 –	"	3	"	12
"	26–27	2 Peter	1	– 29 –	"	4	"	13
"	28	"	2	– 30 –	"	5	"	14

December

The law of his God is in his heart;
none of his steps shall slide

MORNING			Day	EVENING		
1 Chr.	29	2 Peter	3	– 1 –	Micah	6	Luke	15
2 Chr.	1	1 John	1	– 2 –	"	7	"	16
"	2	"	2	– 3 –	Nah.	1	"	17
"	3–4	"	3	– 4 –	"	2	"	18
"	5–6:11	"	4	– 5 –	"	3	"	19
"	6:12–42	"	5	– 6 –	Hab.	1	"	20
"	7	2 John	1	– 7 –	"	2	"	21
"	8	3 John	1	– 8 –	"	3	"	22
"	9	Jude	1	– 9 –	Zeph.	1	"	23
"	10	Rev.	1	– 10 –	"	2	"	24
"	11–12	"	2	– 11 –	"	3	John	1
"	13	"	3	– 12 –	Haggai	1	"	2
"	14–15	"	4	– 13 –	"	2	"	3
"	16	"	5	– 14 –	Zech.	1	"	4
"	17	"	6	– 15 –	"	2	"	5
"	18	"	7	– 16 –	"	3	"	6
"	19–20	"	8	– 17 –	"	4	"	7
"	21	"	9	– 18 –	"	5	"	8
"	22–23	"	10	– 19 –	"	6	"	9
"	24	"	11	– 20 –	"	7	"	10
"	25	"	12	– 21 –	"	8	"	11
"	26	"	13	– 22 –	"	9	"	12
"	27–28	"	14	– 23 –	"	10	"	13
"	29	"	15	– 24 –	"	11	"	14
"	30	"	16	– 25 –	"	12–13:1	"	15
"	31	"	17	– 26 –	"	13:2–9	"	16
"	32	"	18	– 27 –	"	14	"	17
"	33	"	19	– 28 –	Mal.	1	"	18
"	34	"	20	– 29 –	"	2	"	19
"	35	"	21	– 30 –	"	3	"	20
"	36	"	22	– 31 –	"	4	"	21

If you have any questions about this book or Helen's first book, *What Do YOU Want, Lord?* or if you would like further copies of either book, and cannot find them in your local Christian bookshop, please write to the following address:

Doug & Helen Reed
PO Box 434
Tai Po Post Office
Hong Kong